Volume 1
Number 3
Winter 1991

D I A S P O R A

Diaspora (ISSN 1044-2057) is published three times a year by Oxford University Press, 200 Madison Ave., New York, NY 10016. It is sponsored by the Zoryan Institute of Cambridge, MA. Its publication is made possible by the generous support of Kourken Sarkissian.

Subscriptions. The rates for volume 1 (1991) are $23 for individuals and $46 for institutions. Outside the U.S. the rates are $30 for individuals and $53 for institutions; please add $5 for air-expedited delivery. Single copies and back issues are $8.95 for individuals and $16 for institutions. Subscription orders, single-copy orders, change-of-address notifications, and claims for missing copies should be directed to the Journals Department, Oxford University Press, 2001 Evans Road, Cary, NC 27513.

Advertising and permissions. Advertising inquiries and requests to reprint material from the journal should be directed to the Journals Department, Oxford University Press, 200 Madison Ave., New York, NY 10016. The journal is registered with the Copyright Clearance Center, 27 Congress Street, Salem, MA 01970. Microfilm and microfiche inquiries should be directed to University Microfilms Inc., 300 North Zeeb Rd., Ann Arbor, MI 48106.

Postmaster: Send address changes to *Diaspora*, Journals Department, Oxford University Press, 2001 Evans Road, Cary, NC 27513. Printed on acid-free paper effective with Vol. 1, No. 1.

In This Issue,

Apter offers a searching though sympathetic critique of the anthropological paradigm of syncretism, first used by Melville Herskovitz to "measure" the relative purity of retained African elements in the New World diasporas and to fashion a narrative of original cultural unity fragmented by slavery. Challenging the assumptions underpinning this narrative, Apter argues for greater continuity between West Africa and the African diaspora. He locates within West African religious discourse tactics of refiguration and revision that endure in New World diasporas as a collective, counterhegemonic strategy of discursive appropriation.

Scott also turns to Herskovits's "inaugural problematic." Identifying it as the "cornerstone of an anthropology of African diasporas," he identifies its self-appointed task, that of uncovering continuities between Africa and its diaspora. This task persists yet is transformed in the work of Richard Price on the Saramaka, where it takes the form of an attempt to corroborate diasporan memories of originary events. Scott argues that such anthropological discourse seeks to secure authentic collective identity by constructing continuity with the past, and risks neglecting the indispensable work of describing the "local networks of power and knowledge" in which versions of the past are employed to refashion contemporary identities.

Naficy argues that for Iranian exiles living in "Los Angeles or other diasporan communities . . . in highly mediated postindustrial societies . . . , the popular culture they produce and consume, especially television," continually reconstructs and circulates collective identity. He explores the ways in which the rituals of exilic nostalgia draw on preexilic poems and films for images of absence, lack, loss, and return, and stage symbolic reunions. Naficy outlines the boundary-maintaining practices with which exile communities emphasize their difference, claim continuity with their past, and enhance internal similarities. Finally, he explores the ways in which semiotic and ideological power struggles among Iranian factions inflect the process of imagining exile community.

Bottomley brings together three theoretical positions that contribute to a more nuanced study of ethnicity. Pierre Bourdieu's work on the habitus, with its emphasis on a sense of place in historical and social space, and on knowledge embodied in practice, is not usually conjoined with Stuart Hall on ethnicity and Paul Gilroy on diaspora. However, Bottomley teases out of their work ideas about subjectivity, subjection, performance, and ethnicity, then briefly indicates how they may help to interpret diasporan cultures, such as the changes taking place in Greek-Australian dance.

Dirlik, a historian of China, writes about two quite different depictions of the nomadic "barbarian's" encounter with "civilization." The core of his essay is a close reading of two representations of the barbarian (one by a South African, the other by a Turkish novelist). Such representations, he shows, are inseparable from conceptions of "civilization," indeed of History. "Barbarians," Dirlik argues, are "the extreme case that illustrates what [also] happens to . . . diasporas, minorities in ghettos, the Others of the nation-state," who are "situated along a continuum within civilization, as the barbarian is beyond its borders." The introduction of the voices of all these Others into an understanding of "our" History, Dirlik argues, is indispensable if we are to avoid not only the barbarous destruction of the Other but our own incarceration in a narrow conception of civilization.

Schnapper's essay will startle some readers of this journal, who will have detected a certain editorial unanimity in opposition to "melting pot" theories. But the distance between any unanimity and intellectual complacency is short; Schnapper's essay is a reminder of other positions. She argues that France has been a country of immigrants for a long time, that national ideology and a commitment to Gallicization have masked this fact, and have even led to a dearth of data for sociologists, which she laments. While favoring immigration, Schnapper (herself of Jewish origin and the daughter of Raymond Aron) argues that France can have "no policy but that of continuing the integration of its foreign populations through its universal institutions," because "no nation can have suicide as a vocation." This article, simultaneously scholarly and, especially in the American context, polemical, will serve in lieu of a "Commentary" essay for this issue.

Arthur reviews two books by D. H. Akenson on the Irish diaspora in South Africa and New Zealand. Together, these argue the need to elaborate a history of a transnational "Anglo-Celtic" culture, the proper understanding of which would alter the historiography of the "British Isles," affect the self-representation of the host countries, and challenge Irish American stereotypes as to who the emigrants were and how they lived. Arthur endorses a caveat of Akenson's that can be salutary for all ethnic history: "If the historical evidence . . . confirms what your grandmother told you, then check, and check again."

Israel's review of a collection of essays on the Sikh diasporas of Britain, Canada, and the United States enumerates a richly suggestive set of issues. These include debates about the speed with which changes at home and new waves of immigration alter the structure, institutions, and assumptions that prevail in a diaspora: the sharpening of a Hindu/Sikh struggle in the Punjab, for example, has given new vehemence to debates about Sikh identity elsewhere. In turn, such new debates retrospectively transform views about and may "do violence to the historical experience" of earlier immigrants.

We are pleased to announce that the Council of Editors of Learned Journals has selected *Diaspora* as the best new journal of 1991.

Herskovits's Heritage: Rethinking Syncretism in the African Diaspora

Andrew Apter
University of Chicago

It is customary, if not mandatory, in contemporary African dias-pora studies to invoke the pioneering spirit of Melville J. Herskovits (1895–1963), whose lifework was dedicated to the repossession of Africa's heritage in the New World.[1] Not that Herskovits was the first to engage in such research. Others before him included W. E. B. Du Bois and Carter G. Woodson, as well as Jean Price-Mars of Haiti, Fernando Ortiz of Cuba, and—more his contemporaries than pre-decessors—Zora Neale Hurston and the Brazilian ethnologists René Ribeiro, Arthur Ramos, and Gilberto Freyre.[2] But Herskovits more than any other scholar posed the African-American connection as a theoretical problem that, in the service of a progressive if intellec-tually circumscribed political agenda, demanded systematic re-search into an unprecedented range of West African and New World cultures. It is not my aim to praise a great ancestor, whose flaws and limitations are as legendary as his virtues, but to assess the relevance of his theoretical program to contemporary African-Amer-ican research. In particular, I will focus on his syncretic paradigm, which continues—even among those who disavow it as crudely es-sentialist or unwittingly racist—to inform the current renaissance in studies of the African diaspora.

There is much that seems wrong, misconceived, and simply out-dated in Herskovits's syncretic paradigm when it is evaluated against the current standards of a more critical anthropology. It is not difficult to see how Herskovits essentialized tribal origins in Africa, perpetuated myths of cultural purity in the New World, over-looked class formation, and developed passive notions of accultura-tion and cultural resistance, all of which distorted the ethnographic record under the guise of an imputed scientific objectivity. But there is also something elusively tenacious about the concept of syncre-tism. Even when critically deconstructed, it somehow slips back into any meaningful discussion of Africanity in the New World. And even as we recognize that "Africa" has been ideologically constructed to create imagined communities in the black Americas—as Guinée in Haitian *Vodoun*, or the nations of Cuban *Santería* and Brazilian

Candomblé—such invented identities cannot be totally severed from their cultural analogues (dare we say origins?) in West Africa. The goal of this essay is to rethink syncretism in a way that does justice to both sides of this methodological divide: to the inventedness (and inventiveness) of New World African identities as well as to their cultural and historical associations with West African peoples. This resolution requires greater clarity about just what it is we are comparing, contextualizing, and historicizing on both sides of the Atlantic, an exercise that gives a new twist to Herskovits's ethnohistorical method and owes its revisionary strategy to some critical lessons that I learned from the Yoruba in Nigeria.[3]

It is perhaps noteworthy that recent studies of "Africanisms" in the Americas, focusing on particular deities like Ogun, on religions like Santería and Vodoun, or even on transatlantic aesthetic and philosophical complexes, have effectively erased syncretism from their lexicons.[4] These excellent studies indeed reveal that there is much more to such New World cultural forms than a blending of two distinct traditions into a hybrid form. Scholarly emphasis has shifted to disclose the nuanced complexities of the historical conditions in which African identities are remembered and forgotten, fractured and fused, invoked, possessed, repossessed, transposed, and reconfigured within rural peasantries, urban centers, immigrant communities, national arenas, even at transnational conferences on, for example, the Yoruba-based *Òrìṣà* tradition.[5] Consistent with this move is a shift away from cultural form toward cultural performance and practice, to traditions in the making rather than those already made, preserved, or retained. These developments are welcome as part of the positive trend in cultural studies, but it is equally clear that nothing as powerful as the syncretic paradigm has arisen from its ashes, resulting in a compelling crisis of representation. In brief, what is Africa's place in the New World? Indeed, what is "Africa"?[6]

Rather than address this rapidly growing literature, I will return to the essentials of Herskovits's syncretic paradigm in order to extract the interpretive kernel from its scientistic shell. This involves a pilgrimage to the classic shrines of New World syncretism where, in Brazilian Candomblé, Cuban Santería, and Haitian Vodoun, African gods embrace Catholic saints to promote new religious empires. I privilege these sites not only because, for Herskovits, they represented the clearest cases of syncretism as such, but because for us, they provide the clearest examples of how African critical practices in the Americas can inform our own research.

1. The Syncretic Paradigm

Herskovits (*Myth* xxii) credited Arthur Ramos as one of the first to employ the concept of syncretism to account for the identification of African deities with Catholic saints in Brazilian Candomblé. Syncretism suggested, for Herskovits, "a pattern of first importance" in the study of Afro-American culture contact and change, the dynamics of which he continued to document and theorize while refining his method over the years. If the scientificity of this method appears contrived today, we should appreciate that Herskovits posed a radical challenge to the sociological interpretations of American and New World "Negro" institutions and practices which, according to E. Franklin Frazier and Robert E. Park (among others), represented functional adaptations to socioeconomic conditions rather than African cultural holdovers or survivals (see Frazier, Park, and Smith). Herskovits called for greater sensitivity to history and culture in the acculturative process, arguing effectively that synchronic sociological reductionism not only violated the ethnographic record, but worse, supported the racist myth that the Negro had no meaningful African history or heritage. It is with this spirit and strategy in mind that his syncretic paradigm must be understood.

Under the rubric of "ethnohistorical method," Herskovits meant simply that ethnology and history should be combined "to recover the predominant regional and tribal origins of the New World Negroes" and "to establish the cultural base-lines from which the processes of change began" (*New World* 49). This baseline, he argued, was restricted to the West African coastal and rain-forest belts, running from Senegal to Angola, since the smaller and later shipments of slaves from East Africa, Mozambique, and Madagascar had minimal cultural impact on previously established West African patterns in the New World. While this claim is debatable, although probably true, it is not my aim to evaluate its empirical plausibility in light of new evidence (e.g., Curtin), but to clarify its underlying logic. In this view, West African cultures are figured as discrete, coherent wholes, which, with varying degrees of purity and in different spheres of social life, left their impress on the black Americas. To assess the relative purity of African retentions and to specify their social domains, Herskovits developed a number of related concepts which together can be glossed as the syncretic paradigm.[7] In addition to the ethnohistorical method, these concepts are: 1) scale of intensity, 2) cultural focus, 3) syncretism proper, 4) reinterpretation, and 5) cultural imponderables. I will review these concepts not only to point out their profound limitations, but also to draw out their theoretical relevance to contemporary diaspora studies.

If Herskovits regarded his scale of intensities as one of his greatest methodological achievements, with hindsight it seems to parody the epistemology of liberal social science. In an effort to quantify New World Africanisms, albeit for heuristic rather than statistical purposes, Herskovits developed a logical continuum from most to least African, segmented into (a) very African, (b) quite African, (c) somewhat African, (d) a little African, (e) trace of African customs, or absent, and (?) no report. These relative values were placed in a two-dimensional array, with New World regions and communities like Guiana (bush and Paramaribo), Haiti (peasant and urban), and the United States (Gullah Islands, rural South, urban North) along a vertical axis, and with specific sociocultural domains (technology, economics, social organization, religion, art, music, etc.) segmented along a horizontal axis to represent variable degrees of African intensity within each region or community. Despite internal variations, the resulting table (Table 1) reveals that "the progression of Guiana, Haiti, Brazil, Jamaica, Trinidad, Cuba, Virgin Islands, the Gullah Islands, and southern and northern United States comprise a series wherein a decreasing intensity of Africanisms is manifest" (*New World* 54). Today, the empirical conclusions can be revised. For example, we know from the Prices' work in Surinam that Guiana is much more creolized than Herskovits ever imagined (see Richard Price, Sally Price, and S. and R. Price). But the conceptual problems of this schema are more serious. Clearly the intensities themselves (such as "very," "quite," and "somewhat African") are highly relative and subjective. Also, the sociocultural domains (social organization, religion, art) are in no way discrete and ignore class divisions, while the regional and community designations are inconsistent with each other. For example, only Haiti is divided into "urban" and "peasant," even though this is a distinction which Bastide has shown to be highly salient in Brazil.

As a form of knowledge, the scale of intensities resembles the anthropometric measures of physical anthropology, which Herskovits deployed in his postdoctoral research on the phenotypical effects of miscegenation in North America (see *American Negro*). Although he was always explicit—following his mentor, Franz Boas—about separating race from culture and language, his scale of intensities echoes a blood-based logic by transposing notions of purity and dilution from racial stocks to cultural genealogies. Thus he could claim that "the Bush Negroes of the Guiana forests manifest African culture *in purer form* than is to be encountered anywhere else outside Africa" (*Myth* 124) and that "rural and urban Negro cultures took on *somewhat different shadings*" (135) (emphasis added), with the darker peasants more African than their lighter, more acculturated urban brothers and sisters. I do not mean to suggest that Herskovits was a closet racist—a rather cheap shot against a scholar whose progressive views were so ahead of his time.[8] But it should remain clear how easily the language of race entered into the discourse of syncretism in the New World, particularly when the rhetoric of science was wedded to essentialized concepts of African culture in comparative studies funded by the Carnegie Corporation.[9]

If the scale of intensities represented variable degrees and do-

Table 1. Scale of Intensities of New World Africanisms

	Tech-nology	Eco-nomic	Social organi-zation	Non-kinship institu-tions	Reli-gion	Magic	Art	Folk-lore	Music	Lan-guage
Guiana (bush)	b	b	a	a	a	a	b	a	a	b
Guiana (Paramaribo)	c	c	b	c	a	a	e	a	a	c
Haiti (peasant)	c	b	b	c	a	a	d	a	a	c
Haiti (urban)	e	d	c	c	b	b	e	a	a	c
Brazil (Bahia-Recife)	d	d	b	d	a	a	b	a	a	a
Brazil (Porto Alegre)	e	e	e	d	a	a	e	a	a	c
Brazil (Maranhao-rural)	c	c	b	e	c	b	e	b	b	d
Brazil (Maranhao-urban)	e	d	c	e	a	b	e	d	a	b
Cuba	e	d	c	b	a	a	b	b	a	a
Jamaica (Maroons)	c	c	b	b	b	a	e	a	a	c
Jamaica (Morant Bay)	e	c	b	b	a	a	e	a	a	a
Jamaica (general)	e	c	d	d	b	b	e	a	b	c
Honduras (Black Caribs)	c	c	b	b	b	a	e	b	c	e
Trinidad (Port of Spain)	e	d	c	b	a	a	e	b	a	e
Trinidad (Toco)	e	d	c	c	c	b	e	b	b	d
Mexico (Guerrero)	d	e	b	b	c	b	e	b	?	e
Colombia (Choco)	d	d	c	c	c	b	e	b	e	e
Virgin Islands	e	d	c	d	e	b	e	b	b	d
U.S. (Gullah Islands)	c	c	c	d	c	b	e	a	b	b
U.S. (rural South)	d	e	c	d	c	b	e	b	b	e
U.S. (urban North)	e	e	c	d	c	b	e	d	b	e

a: very African b: quite African c: somewhat African d: a little African e: trace of African, or none ?: no report

Source: Adapted from Herskovits, *The New World Negro,* 53.

mains of African retention—high for religion, low for economics and art—it offered no explanations. To understand why some practices thrived when and where they did while others went underground or disappeared, Herskovits developed his general theory of syncretism, supplemented by concepts of reinterpretation, cultural focus, and what he called (no doubt echoing Malinowski [20–21]) "cultural imponderables." Narrowly defined, syncretism is produced in situations of contact between cultures from "the tendency to identify those elements in the new culture with similar elements in the old one, enabling the persons experiencing the contact to move from one to the other, and back again, with psychological ease" (Herskovits, *New World* 57). Thus, he notes, in the Catholic New World, African gods are identified with saints of the Church, whereas in Protestant areas the religious associations are more subtle, and African cultural retentions (e.g., mourning and shouting) less intense. We can perceive in this notion a strong psychological emphasis on the individual as syncretic agent, on identification as the syncretic process, and on adaptation and integration ("psychological ease") as syncretic functions, which extend secondarily to groups in their new cultural contexts. The same process occurs, according to Herskovits, "in substance rather than form, in psychological value rather than in name" (*New World* 57) when the resemblance between cultural elements is too weak to afford a fully syncretic relationship but is strong enough to allow a reinterpretation of the new by the old. Herskovits's favorite example of reinterpretation is his claim that African polygyny was retained under monogamous constraints, with his arguing that polygyny was reinterpreted in diachronic terms by the practice of serial unions. This example reveals Herskovits's sociological naïveté in downplaying contemporaneous social conditions in favor of imputed cultural continuities, but the principle itself, I will argue, is extremely salient when recast as a revisionary strategy.

If syncretism and reinterpretation are mainly psychological concepts that explain how the new culture is adopted within the framework of the old, the concept of cultural focus shifts the analysis to culture sui generis. To explain why African religious beliefs and practices in the New World are retained with greater clarity and vigor than, for example, kinship, economic, and political institutions, Herskovits argues that religion itself constitutes the cultural focus of African peoples—their "particular emphasis," "distinguishing flavor," and "essential orientation" (59). That which is given highest cultural priority by a people will offer the greatest "resistance" to change, he argues, and will thus rank high on the scale of New World Africanisms. Therefore culture, by way of its distinguishing focus, plays a determinative role in the selective process of what is and is not retained, in what form, with what degree of intensity, and in what sphere of social life. Thus for Herskovits:

> [M]ore elements which lie in the area of focus of a receiving culture will be retained than those appertaining to other aspects of the culture, acceptance being greater in those phases of culture further removed from the focal area. When a culture is under pressure by a dominant group who seek to induce acceptance of its traditions, elements lying in the focal area will be retained longer than those outside it. . . . (59)

We have no clearer commitment to (a relativized) cultural determinism than in this passage, which provides a rather strange take on the initial socioeconomic context of African culture contact—that of slavery in the New World. Elsewhere Herskovits was clearly aware of the different forms of plantation slavery and the modes of passive and active resistance that the slaves deployed, including foot-dragging, suicide, escape, *maronnage,* and organized revolt (*Myth* 86–109). But here we are led to believe that religion—more than kinship, politics, or economics—persisted in a world that turned Africans into laboring chattel and destroyed their families because it served as the dominant cultural focus. Such a position seems to defy rational argument if not common political sense, displaying what Jackson identifies, in another context, as Herskovits's "curious naivete about the relationship between culture and power" (Jackson, "Herskovits" 144). But even here, I will argue, lies the germ of an idea that helps to explain the power of syncretic practices in real and effective terms. I will argue that the hermeneutical principles of West African religions—particularly Yoruba religion, which has thrived in various New World guises—have provided salient forms of popular resistance in a variety of oppressive conditions.

The final concept in Herskovits's syncretic paradigm—that of cultural imponderables—introduces the variable dimension of consciousness in African diaspora research and prefigures the study of practical and embodied knowledge in current anthropology. For in addition to consciously retained Africanisms emanating from the cultural core, Herskovits discerned a range of "retentions" that "are carried below the level of consciousness" (*New World* 59) and persist in everyday practices. These include the linguistic patterns of accents, dialects, and creoles; the musical styles of, for instance, Son, Rumba, Mambo, and Blues; the "motor habits" of expressive gestures and dance; and the "codes of etiquette" which inform greetings and politeness formulae. At a time when such phenomena were often explained in racist terms, as transmitted through blood, Herskovits took great pains to emphasize their cultural character, as acquired by successive generations. More interesting for us, how-

ever, was his understanding that such culturally embodied imponderables persisted as retentions because they resisted change.
Clearly, this notion of resistance is passive, attributed elsewhere to
"the force of cultural conservatism" (57), and is conceived nega-
tively, as the absence of assimilation. But as we shall see, when
"updated," this notion foreshadows theories of active resistance that
identify bodily practices as contested sites of symbolic and ideological struggle (Comaroff and Comaroff 24–25).

Thus reduced to its essentials, Herskovits's syncretic paradigm
highlights the limitations of American liberal scholarship. In retro-
spect, its major features—the racist overtones of the scale of intensities; the psychologistic orientation of syncretism and reinterpretation, which privilege adaptation and accommodation over
opposition and contradiction; the absence of any sustained class
analysis; the emphasis on an inertial cultural focus over and above
the dialectics of power and identity construction; and finally, the
essentially conservative vision of cultural retention as that which
resists change—all seem to relegate Herskovits to a dubious past.
Having dissected the syncretic paradigm to critique its component
parts, highlighting their limitations while flagging their redeeming
features for later discussion, I will now turn to the paradigm as a
whole in its more substantive applications, in order to interrogate
the notion of cultural origins that informs the syncretic process.

2. Deconstructing Origins

In Herskovits's "African Gods and Catholic Saints in New World
Negro Belief," first published in *American Anthropologist* (1937), we
find the official liberal blueprint of the science of New World syncretisms, based on fieldwork in Haiti as well as on published Cuban
and Brazilian data. To be sure, Herskovits was one of the first North
American anthropologists to recognize the validity—indeed the
privileged status—of Caribbean societies as objects of ethnographic
study, at a time when the discipline preferred "pristine" primitives
in "natural" habitats to cultures reconstituted in "diluted" forms
through slavery or other coercive dislocations. Such settings, he argued, provided "laboratory situations" (*New World* 46) for investi-
gating the dynamics of acculturation—of what is lost, modified, or
retained through culture contact, and the mechanisms that govern
the process.

In this respect, Herskovits perceived the universal significance of
New World syncretisms for the "science of man," in that they provided the clearest cases, given adequate data, of more general principles of culture contact and change the world over. In this view,
New World cultures moved from a marginal ethnographic status to
center stage, and if the assumptions that guided his study appear

simplistic and naïve, distorting (as I shall now illustrate) the very data themselves, the larger conceptual revolution that he inspired linked empirical studies of the African diaspora to a general theory of culture.

According to Herskovits, the syncretic identification of African gods with Catholic saints was shaped by two primary factors in the New World: by slavery as the dominant institution of social life (or, for Orlando Patterson, "social death") and by Catholicism as the official religion of the masters. These two factors together account for the distinctive patterns of syncretism found in Haitian Vodoun, Cuban Santería and Brazilian Candomblé, in that the slaves were summarily baptized as they came off the ships and were thrust into sugar mills and plantations, where they secretly continued to worship their gods under the cloak of official Catholicism. Banned by the authorities, the African cults were forced underground, where they provided a focus for sporadic slave revolts, were uneasily tolerated during Catholic holidays, and fragmented into local groups that were mainly shaped and dominated by the personalities of their leaders (*New World,* Herskovits, 322). I do not have space in this limited review to discuss the complex social, political, and religious variations that historically unfolded, except to mention the most general cultural consequence identified by Herskovits. This is the profound fragmentation of aboriginal African unities, a forced fusion of different African cultures and the dismemberment of religious cult hierarchies into shattered splinter groups, "reflected in a resulting confusion of theological concept" (*New World* 322–23).

It is this model of cultural and theological fragmentation that I will challenge, focusing first on Herskovits's tropes of aboriginal unity. Despite his call for rigor in identifying the numerous cultural origins of New World slaves, Herskovits reduces African influences to two principal sources—Fon and Yoruba.[10] The deities identified with Catholic saints are limited—at least upon first inspection—to the pantheons of these two great West African cultures, such that Fon gods like the trickster Legba, the rainbow-serpent Damballa, and the Marassa twins syncretized with Saint Anthony, Saint Patrick, and the twin saints Cosmas and Damien, while Yoruba gods like the trickster Eshu, the thunder-god Shango, and the water-goddess Yemoja (Yemanja) were similarly identified with the Devil, Saint Barbara, and the Virgen de Regla. The correspondences are based, we may recall, on the similarities of religious elements, such that the saintly icons depicted on Catholic chromolithographs exhibit symbolic features of African counterparts; thus, the serpents on Saint Patrick's image invoke the Fon serpent-deity Damballa, whereas the twin saints Cosmas and Damien resemble the Fon Marassa or Yoruba Ibeji twins. Under repressive conditions of official opprobrium, the slaves—so the argument goes—were able to wor-

243

ship in two worlds at once; outwardly Catholic, inwardly they honored their African gods.

Following this syncretic principle of identification, Herskovits constructed a table of correspondences between African gods and Catholic saints in Brazil, Cuba, and Haiti, listing African deities in a vertical left-hand column with their saintly counterparts to the right (Table 2). Again, it is not the specific correspondences that I will challenge (since as Herskovits perceived, these vary both regionally and over time), but the table itself as a form of knowledge and the assumptions embedded within it. For these amount to a specific discursive modality, a way of constructing African identities and differences, of figuring (or as Mudimbe might say, conjugating) Africanity in the New World as an acculturative process. And it is this discourse that can be fruitfully deconstructed, not abstractly from the lofty heights of postmodern criticism, but concretely, on the basis of internal evidence supplemented by empirical data from Nigeria.

First, I would call attention to a subtle but powerful slippage subsumed by the category of the left-hand column—that of "African deities," wherein several significant contrasts are neutralized. Following the logic of the syncretic paradigm, "Africa" refers to a West African baseline, an ethnohistorical reality circumscribed by space and time and identified as the source of African influence in the New World. Here the Fon and Yoruba figure as dominant cultural origins (with Congo receiving a passing reference associated with Haitian Simbi deities), since either Fon or Yoruba deities can be identified with Catholic saints. But here is where the cultural waters get muddied, for apart from a few central deities like the Fon Damballa and the Yoruba Ibeji, it is impossible to distinguish the two religious pantheons as culturally discrete. I will not recount the complex history of Dahomean-Yoruba political relations, except to mention that from at least the sixteenth century (and probably earlier) through the mid-nineteenth century, warfare, slave-raiding, migration, and ritual reciprocity between the kingdoms of Dahomey, Ketu, and Old Oyo persisted, with much cultural mixing of religious deities and institutions (see Akinjogbin, Law, and Parrinder). There is a general historiographic tendency to see Yoruba gods like Ogun (of war and iron) and Ifa (of divination) recoded in Dahomey as Gu and Fa, suggesting a regional Yoruba diaspora to the west. But one equally finds the Yoruba trickster Eshu referred to as Eshu-Elegba as far east as the Ekiti region of Yorubaland, suggesting a complementary infusion of Fon deities into Yoruba pantheons. My point is not to argue which gods came from where—a possible and quite valuable regional exercise within limited terms—but to challenge the aboriginal purity of Herskovits's tribal baseline. In brief, Fon and Yoruba are not pure cultural categories. Indeed, the very notion of a singular Yoruba people was a missionary invention of the mid-nineteenth century, subsuming Egba, Egbado, Ijebu, Ijesha, and Ekiti peoples, among others, to a standardized Oyo-Yoruba linguistic and cultural model.

Whether wittingly or not, Herskovits avoids this problem of interposed origins by lumping them under the general category of African. His table of correspondences erases the difference between Fon and Yoruba, which remains implicit in the names of certain deities, but which also remains highly ambiguous. The baseline is thus occluded by the trope of aboriginal Africa, grounding a primordial cultural genealogy that quickly vanishes into an unknown past. Nor does systematic slippage stop here. If we examine the left-hand column further, we find "African" deities such as la Sirène, *loa* Christalline, *loa* St. Pierre, *loa* Kpanyol (the Spaniard), Maitresse Erzulie, and 'Ti Jean Petro (little John Petro), deities that never did or could exist in precontact West Africa because they represent European mythic and historical allusions and social stereotypes.

Part of this problem lies with Herskovits's failure to distinguish what he as an external observer and trained anthropologist calls African from what Haitians, Brazilians, and Cubans call African. The table of correspondences confuses both perspectives under "Africa," merging the "etic" with the "emic." Thus Herskovits notes:

> The Haitian . . . does not merely stop at identifying the saints with African gods, for saints are occasionally themselves conceived as *loa* . . . thus St. Louis, the patron of the town of Mirebalais where this field work was carried on, is a *loa* in his own right. Similarly two of the kings who figure in the *image* that depicts the Adoration of the Christ Child, Balthazar and Gaspar, are also held to be *vodun* deities. (*New World* 325)

Before proposing a more critical solution to this problem, it is enough to point out that Herskovits has failed, in the terms established by his syncretic paradigm and table of correspondences, to clearly distinguish cultural origins and African deities from their reconstructed and syncretic forms. The ethnohistorical baseline remains a myth of African origins, not a documented or even documentable point of empirical departure. This myth is significant not only as a foundational fiction, but because it was elaborated by Herskovits in substantive claims that have continued to misguide much New World research.

This brings me to the second tropic function of aboriginal unity, that of coherent, unified, and standardized theologies and pantheons in West Africa that were uprooted and fragmented through the slave trade to be reconstituted in locally variable and confused forms in the Catholic New World. I call this elaboration tropic because it

Table 2. Correspondence between African Gods and Catholic Saints in Brazil, Cuba, and Haiti

African deities as found in:	Brazil	Cuba	Haiti
Obatala		Virgen de las Mercedes; the Most Sacred Sacrament; Christ on the Cross	
Obatala; Orisala; Orixala (Oxala)	'Nosso Senhor do Bomfim' at Bahia; St. Anne; 'Senhor do Bomfim' at Rio (because of the influence of Bahia).		St. Anne
Grande Mambo Batala	St. Barbara at Bahia; St. Michael the Archangel at Rio; St. Jerome (the husband of St. Barbara) at Bahia		
Shango		St. Barbara	
Elegbara, Elegua, Alegua Legba		'Animas benditas del Purgatorio'; 'Anima Sola'	St. Anthony; St. Peter
Exu	the Devil St. George at Rio; St. Jerome; St. Anthony at Bahia		
Ogun		St. Peter	
Ogun Balandjo Ogun Ferraille			St. James the Elder; St. Joseph St. James
Oxun	Virgin Mary; N.D. de Candeias Virgin Mary; N.S. de Rosario (at Bahia); N. D. De Conceicao (Rio)	Virgin de la Caridad del Cobre	
Yemanja		Virgin de Regla	
Maitresse Erzulie; Erzilie; Erzilie Freda Dahomey			Holy Virgin (of the Nativity); Santa Barbara; Mater Dolorosa

Saponam	The Sacred Sacrament		
Osa-Ose (Oxossi)	St. George at Bahia; St. Sebastian at Rio	St. Alberto; St. Hubert	St. John the Baptist
Ololu; Omolu	St. Bento		
Agomme Tonnere		St. John the Baptist	
Ibeji (Brazil and Cuba); Marassa (Haiti)	St. Cosmas and Damien		St. Cosmas and Damien
Father of the Marassa			St. Nicholas
Orunbila (Orunmila)	St. Francisco	St. Francisco	
Loco			
Babayu Ayi		St. Lazarus	
Ifa	The Most Sacred Sacrament		
Yansan (wife of Shango)	St. Barbara (wife of St. Jerome)		
Damballa			St. Patrick
Father of Damballa			Moses
Pierre d'Ambala			St. Peter
loa St. Pierre			St. Peter
Agwe			St. Expeditius
Roi d'Agoueseau			St. Louis (King of France)
Daguy Bologuay			St. Joseph
la Sirene			the Assumption; N.D. de Grace
loa Christalline			St. Philomena
Adamisu Wedo			St. Anne
loa Kpanyol			N.D. de Alta Gracia
Aizan			Christ (?)
Simbi			St. Andrew
Simbi en Deaux Eaux			St. Anthony the Hermit
Azaka Meda			St. Andrew (?)
'Ti Jean Petro			St. Anthony the Hermit

Source: Adapted from Herskovits, *The New World Negro*, 327–28.

establishes a nostalgic topos of a theological Golden Age that never existed in West Africa and should be abandoned as a comparative standard for studying New World religions. The general idea derives from Herskovits's discovery that *Vodoun* theology is highly inconsistent. He found

> differences of opinion not only from region to region, but within a given region even between members of the same group concerning such details of cult belief and practice as the names of deities, modes of ritual procedure, or the genealogies of the gods, to say nothing of concepts regarding the powers and attributes of the African spirits in relation to one another and to the total pantheon. (323)

Eliciting lists of deities from a single Haitian valley, he discovered that "the differences between these lists were much greater than the resemblances; and . . . in identifying deities with Catholic saints, an even greater divergence of opinion was found" (323). The same indeterminacies and patterns of variation apply, on a larger scale, to the African pantheons and their syncretic manifestations in Brazilian Candomblé and Cuban Santería, summarized by the table of correspondences.

It is not the indeterminate character of Herskovits's data that I would challenge but his inference that a greater uniformity ever existed in West Africa. It is in fact the very idea of listing African deities as discrete mystical entities, in fixed relations within pantheons associated with stable sociological correlates on the ground, that my own research on Yoruba òrìṣà worship undermines. Yoruba deities are not only vested in lineages (what Bascom, following Herskovits, called "sib-based" cults), but articulate with more inclusive corporate groups (Bascom's "multi-sib cults"), such as quarters (àdúgbò), each ruled by a town chief, or in the case of royal cults, the town or kingdom as a whole (ìlú). Thus, in a crude sense, the ritual configuration of òrìṣà cults within any kingdom represents its dominant relations of political segmentation, the patterns of which vary spatially, from one kingdom to another, and within kingdoms over time, accommodating (and on important occasions, precipitating) political fission, fusion, or the reranking of civil chiefs (see Bascom, Barber, and Apter ch. 2, 3). The methodological implication of this politico-ritual complementarity—a very gross reduction of a complex dialectic—is that no two Yoruba kingdoms arrange their pantheon of òrìṣà in the same way. The situation is further complicated by the fact that within kingdoms, the òrìṣà cults of different town quarters organize their pantheons around their own principal deities, so that if, officially, a civil chief pays ritual obeisance to the superior òrìṣà of the town king, secretly, within the confines of his own quarter's cult, the chief and his followers recognize the hidden paramountcy of their òrìṣà, around which their pantheon revolves (Apter ch. 6).

The cosmological principles that render such polyvocalities possible and intelligible are grounded in Yoruba notions of "deep knowledge" (*imọ jinlẹ̀*), referring to the privileged access of powerful priests and priestesses to hidden truths and secrets. I will return to the power of such knowledge in due course. For now, it is enough to point out that within this ritually safeguarded space of interpretive possibilities, official dynasties and genealogies are revised, deities are repositioned to express rival political claims, and the deities themselves are fragmented and fused into multiple and singular identities. Small wonder that Herskovits had trouble with his lists, since even in Nigeria, no òrìṣà cult, community, or Yoruba kingdom (let alone two individuals) would produce the same list or pantheon of òrìṣà.

From this stems a second dominant misconception—that òrìṣà cults in West Africa represent discrete deities, with one cult worshipping Shango, another Yemoja, a third Obatala, and so on. In fact, all òrìṣà cults house clusters of deities that are represented by specific priests and priestesses, altars, and sacrifices, and are grafted onto an apical deity.[11] Within these microarenas, the configuration of these clustered deities also shifts with changes in the status of their associated lineages and titled representatives and according to contesting claims from within. Under these conditions, no definitive list of deities is possible. More significant for syncretic models is the mistaken claim—and here Bastide and Verger keep company with Herskovits—that formerly discrete cults in Africa were restructured, in the New World, to house a multiplicity of African deities and Catholic saints. The ethnohistorical record reveals that Yoruba òrìṣà cults were never discrete in the first place.

Zora Neale Hurston was one of the first to grasp the elusive polymorphism of the Haitian loa in her more personal (and in many ways proto-experimental) ethnography of Vodoun, understanding that "*No one* knows the name of every *loa* because every major section of Haiti has its own variation" (*Tell* 114), and that the loa themselves are both multiple and singular. My point has been to extend this indeterminacy back to southwest Nigeria where Yoruba religion reveals much greater continuity with its syncretic manifestations than Herskovits ever imagined. The theological confusion in New World cults and pantheons which for Herskovits resulted from the upheavals of slavery is actually endemic to òrìṣà worship (and I suspect to Fon religion as well) and resolves into a critical hermeneutics of power, once its relevant dimensions are grasped. In thus reformulating Herskovits's ideas, we will see that he was onto something very important. He concluded his seminal comparison of Brazilian, Cuban, and Haitian syncretisms with the observation that, despite the confusion surrounding African deities and their Catholic correspondences, a general syncretic process was at work:

> Considered as a whole . . . the data show quite clearly to what extent *the inner logic* of the aboriginal African cultures of the Negroes, when brought in contact with foreign traditions, worked out to achieve an end that, despite the handicaps of slavery, has been relatively the same wherever the forces for making change have been comparable. (328) (emphasis added)

It is this inner logic, recast as a cultural hermeneutics, that provides the key to understanding the West African contribution to New World syncretic forms and does so without recourse to foundational fictions of essentialized aboriginal unity.

3. From Syncretic to Critical Practice

Thus far I have deconstructed Herskovits's myth of African origins—its figures of cultural purity, theological unity, lineage-based cult organization, and cult singularity (i.e., one deity per ritual collectivity)—in order to extract the interpretive kernel from its ideological shell. If Herskovits distorted the West African baseline with misconceptions that can be scrapped or readjusted, he also established the ground of a cultural argument that can be further developed. The goal of this argument, as I mentioned earlier, is to determine what is African in the African diaspora, focusing on religious syncretism as a clear case of Africanity in order to theorize its subtler forms of influence in the New World.

First, however, we must acknowledge that the trope of "Africa" has served as a dominant ideological category in the service of empire, a category that has naturalized, as Mudimbe (*Invention*) so cogently demonstrates, the normative and territorial dominions of Europe's "civilizing mission" (see also Comaroff and Comaroff 86–125). But it must also be emphasized that a deconstruction of this master trope, as Mudimbe's radical project demands, does not do justice to the other side, to that which lies beyond the ideological limits of an Africa produced by missionary-colonial discourse. This other side of Africa must not be taken to refer to the fiction of pristine cultures stipulated by Herskovits, but neither is it reducible to some unknowable Other in a move that annihilates the very histories of peoples who have come to define themselves as Africans with specific national and ethnic identities. If African worlds are as much the constructs of Africanist discourses as the objects of their inquiry, then it is within this dialectic of invention and observation that the concept of syncretism performs a double synthesis. In brief,

Africa is assimilated to the New World through culture contact if and only if an invented Africa is assimilated to an Africa observed. We are caught in a double bind. Either we essentialize Africa or renounce it.

One way out of this ideological dilemma is to focus on the inner logic of syncretic practices as strategies of appropriation and empowerment. What Haitian Vodoun, Brazilian Candomblé and Cuban Santería have in common is a history of accommodation and resistance, not merely in the cultural terms of allying uneasily with Catholicism but also in the political contexts of class division and the state. It is precisely this relation between implicit social knowledge and political economy—what in my Yoruba research has emerged as a hermeneutics of power—that defines the horizon of Africanity in the New World: not as core values or cultural templates but as dynamic and critical practices.

Nowhere is this critical relation between forms of knowledge and relations of domination more evident than in the history of Haitian Vodoun. The conventional historiography traces a grand development from the late eighteenth century to the regime of François Duvalier ("Papa Doc"), over the course of which Vodoun's original revolutionary impulse was gradually co-opted by the state. Thus in 1791, rites conducted by the famous *houngan* (priest) Boukman inspired the first organized blow against the French plantocracy (see Courlander). According to Haitian historical memory, it was in a clearing of the Bois Caiman that, "under a raging tropical downpour accompanied by lightning and the cracking of giant trees, [Boukman] performed a Petro ceremony" in which "a pig was sacrificed and its blood, mixed with gunpowder, was distributed among participants to strengthen their will to win" (Bastien 42).[12] The revolutionary triumvirate of Toussaint L'Ouverture, Jean-Jacques Dessalines, and Henri Christophe were quick to capitalize on Vodoun's popular appeal and its secret channels of communication in mobilizing the masses. Hence it is generally accepted that Vodoun played a strategic role in achieving Haitian independence. After the revolution's success in 1804, however, Vodoun played into the hands of both the center and the opposition. In his efforts to stabilize the new government, Dessalines allied with the mulatto elite and tried to foster Catholicism. He was murdered in 1806 and then resurrected as a *loa*, thereby incorporated into the very pantheon of deities that as official leader he had grown to oppose. His successor, Christophe, suffered a similar reversal. As king of northern Haiti until his suicide in 1820, he encouraged Catholicism as the official religion of state administration and alienated himself from the peasantry. Subsequent Haitian leaders, such as the self-proclaimed Emperor Faustin Soulouque (1847–59), cultivated alliances and reputations among the houngan and their followers while paying official lip-service to Catholicism. Under Antoine Simon (1906–11), for example, the National Palace was recognized as a sacred site of Vodoun activities.

Thus in the first century of Haitian independence, Vodoun articulated with a complex set of emerging political and class divisions. Centralized government favored Catholicism as the official religion of administration, based in the urban centers of Cap Haitien, the northern seat of black elite power, and in Port-au-Prince, the southern seat of the mulattos. Vodoun remained a predominantly rural religion of the black peasantry, providing a powerful political resource for black leaders like Soulouque, who could play the peasantry against the mulatto elite by invoking the popular religion of the people. In this postcolonial context, the religious syncretism of Vodoun and Catholicism played into the dialectics of class and color stratification. As Catholicism spread into the countryside and merged with Vodoun, the latter seeped, as it were, into the palace, providing unofficial access to leadership and state power. This trend was not constant, since Vodoun was periodically attacked by mulatto leaders who allied, after 1860, with the Vatican and waged at times brutal campaigns against the houngan. But these campaigns only reinforced the black opposition, which eventually united under Duvalier into a deadly combination of Vodoun, noirisme, nationalism, and state power.

The stage for Duvalier's appropriation was prepared by the American occupation of Haiti (1915–43), which inspired Haitian intellectuals like Jean Price-Mars to rediscover within Vodoun the "genius" of the Haitian people in his celebration of *negritude*. Formerly disdained by the educated elites, Vodoun was suddenly elevated in the respectable language of poetry and folklore to the status of national heritage and identity (Derby). Leftist intellectuals allied with the peasantry to demand an authentic and truly autonomous Haiti. It was in such an atmosphere that Papa Doc appropriated Vodoun to consolidate dictatorial control. As a peasant religion, Vodoun mobilized enough popular support to counterbalance mulatto and church opposition; as a symbol of Haitian nationalism, it appealed to leftist intellectuals and noiristes; and with its underground network of secret Bizongo and Secte Rouge societies (Davis 241–284), it provided an ideal channel for administering state power and terror while effectively dividing all organized opposition to the self-proclaimed President-For-Life.

It appears that the history of Haitian Vodoun is a history of popular resistance and state appropriation—of the high and official appropriating the low and popular—in that the religion which originally inspired revolution came to uphold a dictatorial state. In a basic sense this is true, but what is lost in such an instrumental interpretation is how Vodoun and its associated notions of Africanity (Guinée) have mediated the complex dialectics of political competition and class division. To be sure, Vodoun remained a powerful resource in the hands of revolutionary leaders and shrewd politicians and has clearly made a difference in Haitian history. But what has made Vodoun so powerful? Strategic explanations that it mobilized collective action only beg the question of how this was done.

At this point, I would like to tie the various threads of this discussion together, rethinking syncretism in the African diaspora as a critical and revisionary practice, one that reconfigures dominant discourses with variable, and at times quite significant, consequences. Haiti provides the clearest illustration that resistance waged through syncretic struggle—through the appropriation by African powers of Catholic saints, postrevolutionary kings, and nationalist rhetoric—was more than symbolic wish fulfillment. But it also illustrates the other side of syncretism, in that the dominant categories which were semantically revised were also, in more formal terms, reproduced and perpetuated.[13] If Vodoun took possession of Catholic hierarchies through the very gods that possessed their devotees, it also reproduced the authoritative structure of God the Father and his saintly messengers, disseminating popular Catholicism throughout the countryside. It was this double aspect of syncretism that Herskovits identified as an acculturative process, as the uneasy adaptation of cultures in collision. What Herskovits missed was the critical relation between cultural form and hegemony, although he intuited the variable modalities that this relation could take.

Returning to the classic syncretism of African gods and Catholic saints, we can recast its historical genesis as a grand counterhegemonic strategy. What Herskovits perceived as a psychological mechanism of cultural integration, allowing blacks to move between African and colonial orders with relative conceptual and emotional ease, was in fact a much more powerful process of discursive appropriation. If in Haiti, as in Cuba and Brazil, the dominant discourse of Catholicism baptized Africans into slavery, it was also Africanized through syncretic associations to establish black nations, identities, and idioms of resistance. The role of Vodoun in the Haitian revolution may stand out for its outstanding impact, but parallel developments occurred throughout the New World. Thus in Brazil, the *quilombos* and *mocambos,* or black republics of escaped slaves, began as religious protest movements which Africanized Portuguese Catholicism along various ethnic lines. Palmares, the largest and most famous of the quilombos, recreated Bantu models of social organization and government, combining African effigies with Catholic icons in its shrines as early as 1645 (Bastide 83–90). And in Cuba, the 1844 slave revolt called *La Escalera*—so named to commemorate the ladders to which the vanquished slaves were tied and tortured—grew out of "an elaborate conspiracy in Matanzas, organized through the *cabildos* and drum dances of the sugar estates, the 'king' and 'queen' of the weekly dance being the agents of conspiracy" (Thomas 205). I mention these famous uprisings not merely to illustrate a strategic relationship between slave religion and organized revolt but to argue that the power of syncretic revision was real and that when conditions were right, the African communities thus imagined and organized asserted themselves with considerable impact.

The syncretic revision of dominant discourses sought to transform the authority that these discourses upheld. To be sure, radical ruptures were exceptional and stand out in Caribbean history as memorable flashpoints in the perduring black struggle. But the general point I wish to emphasize is that the power and violence mobilized by slave revolts and revolution were built into the logic of New World syncretism itself. The Catholicism of Vodoun, Candomblé and Santería was not an ecumenical screen, hiding the worship of African deities from official persecution. It was the religion of the masters, revised, transformed, and appropriated by slaves to harness its power within their universes of discourse. In this way the slaves took possession of Catholicism and thereby repossessed themselves as active spiritual subjects. Nor was this revisionary strategy specific to slavery; it developed also under subsequent conditions of class and color stratification, among black rural peasantries and urban proletariats (see Bastide). The political dimensions of such syncretic revision began not with social protest and calls to arms but with the unmaking of hegemony itself. As Carnival and possession rituals so clearly illustrate, this is accomplished by reversing high and low categories with blacks above whites in the Africanized streets and shrines, by recentering Catholic hierarchies around African gods, by reinscribing ritual space with palm fronds, crossroads, and kingly thrones, by marking time to different drum rhythms and ritual calendars, and by liberating the body from its disciplined constraints (see DaMatta, Parker, and Alonso). Possession by spirits—which include Catholic saints as well as African deities, for even these two orders ritually collapse—involves sexual transgression and gender crossing because it transcends and transforms the most fundamental categories of the natural and social worlds.

But if hegemony is unmade through syncretic ritual, it is also remade, and it would be wrong to equate its religious impulse with protorevolutionary struggle pure and simple. As noted earlier, the ritual revision of dominant discourses also reproduces their grammar and syntax, which it reconstructs from below. In Vodoun, this unmaking and remaking of hegemony corresponds to two sets of spiritual powers: the cool Rada deities of the right hand (often traced back to Allada in Dahomey), who sanction authority, and the hot Petro deities of the left hand (identified as chthonic), who lampoon and decenter the status quo. In Brazilian Candomblé and Cuban Santería, as in Yoruba òrìṣà worship, both types of power inhabit one general pantheon and associate with cool and hot deities such as Obatala and Shango. One can trace the permutations of this basic opposition through innumerable examples, but the point I wish to highlight is that syncretism necessarily involves both the unmaking and remaking of hegemony and thus is intrinsically political.

Returning to Herskovits's syncretic paradigm and locating it within a context of cultural hegemony, we can reduce its basic concepts to a more general dialectic of revision and reproduction. Those things Herskovits reified into categorical distinctions—between syncretism proper, reinterpretation, cultural focus, and embodied forms of expressive culture—reflect variable modalities of cultural resistance, not in his passive sense of resisting change but actively, as counterhegemonic strategy. By appropriating the categories of the dominant classes, ranging from official Catholicism to more nuanced markers of social status and cultural style and by resisting the dominant disciplines of bodily reform through the "hysterical fits" (Larose 86) of spiritual possession, New World blacks empowered their bodies and souls to remake their place within Caribbean societies. As we have seen, the material consequences of these revisionary strategies range from negligible to revolutionary, from the spiritual nationalism asserted, for example, by Vodoun sword-flags brandished before the National Palace, to the self-conscious nationalism of Jean Price-Mars, reclaiming Vodoun as the model of negritude, to the Haitian revolution itself. And as we have also noted, the power of revisionary challenges from below could be reappropriated by the elites, in the academic folklore of Fernando Ortiz and Gilberto Freyre, or in the Machiavellian statecraft of Duvalier. There is no single trajectory of exalted class struggle built into syncretic forms of revision and resistance, or vice versa (as has been suggested for Haiti). What concerns us is the hermeneutics of revision as such and the interpretive conditions of its possibility.

This final concern brings us back to our initial inquiry into what is properly African in the African diaspora. I have deconstructed Herskovits's essentialized cultural baseline, its trope of an aboriginal Golden Age, and its attendant reifications of cultural purity and dilution, without renouncing the logic of cultural genealogies. I will conclude by making my position explicit, by establishing the historically critical relationship between West Africa and the New World.

Boldly stated, the revisionary power of the syncretic religions derives from West African hermeneutical traditions which disseminated through the slave trade and took shape in black communities to remake the New World in the idioms of the old. It is not the elements of Old and New World cultures that should be meaningfully juxtaposed in the concept of syncretism—as Herskovits maintained—but the orthodox and heterodox discourses in which such elements have been deployed and the tropic operations that they have performed. I have dwelt perhaps excessively on refiguration and revision because these are the strategies that have made, and continue to make, a difference—rhetorical, pragmatic, and, in key moments, political—among blacks, mulattos, and whites in the Americas (see Gates). These are also the discursive strategies that characterize West African religions, particularly Yoruba religion, which has had a long history of reconfiguring hegemony, documentable from the rise and fall of the Old Oyo empire (1600–1836), through the nineteenth century Yoruba wars, to the appropriation of Christian and colonial rhetoric in Nigeria's long march to independence. Thus West Africa's contribution to the African diaspora lies not merely in specific ritual symbols and forms, but also in the interpretive practices that generate their meanings. In Yoruba cosmology, for example, deep knowledge (imọ jinlẹ̀) has no determinate content but rather safeguards a space for opposing hegemony. Sanctioned by ritual and safeguarded by secrecy, deep knowledge claims are invoked to revise dynastic genealogies, the rankings of civil chiefs, and even the relative positions of deities within official pantheons. Deep knowledge by definition opposes public discourse, and the authoritative taxonomies that it upholds—whatever they may be. If this is what has made West African religions powerful in relation to local, colonial, and postcolonial hegemonies, it has also informed syncretic revisions of dominant hierarchies in the New World, incorporating them within more popular pantheons and cosmological fields of command.

The concepts of syncretism, reinterpretation, and cultural imponderables, which for Herskovits distinguished different types of African retentions, are recast in my argument as modalities of revision and resistance. I have traced them back not to a pristine cultural baseline but to a dynamic variety of West African interpretive strategies, thereby revising Herskovits's concept of cultural focus into a more critical concept of cultural hermeneutics. If I seem to have succumbed to the indeed substantial hegemony of Yoruba chauvinism in black diaspora debates, it is not to assert that Yoruba cosmology has had the greatest impact in the New World, although its impact has been and remains profound, but because its hermeneutical principles of refiguration and revision are so clearly at work in the classic syncretic religions and illuminate their power. I have restricted my discussion to Herskovits's ethnohistorical project (which, if groundbreaking in its time, appears narrow next to current research on colonial mimesis, public culture, and transnational

identity) because within this more global set of issues, it reminds us
that even after they are deconstructed, the Old World origins of the
African diaspora can be recovered and their heritage explored in
endless depth.

Notes

This essay was first presented at the African Studies Public Lecture Series, Northwestern University, 28 Oct. 1991. I would like to thank David Cohen, Ivan Karp, Karin Hansen, Bill Murphy, and Teju Olaniyan for their challenging and insightful comments.

1. The term "New World," which denotes the post-Columbus Americas, is full of ideological problems all the more pressing in this quincentennial year. I retain the term uneasily for the sake of historiographic continuity, with the qualification that invisible quotes surround each of my usages to bracket its pejorative connotations.

2. See, for example, Du Bois; Woodson; Price-Mars; Ortiz; Hurston, *Tell My Horse;* Ribeiro; Ramos; and Freyre.

3. The Nigerian fieldwork on which this argument is based took place from October 1982 to December 1984 and during three months of summer 1990. I gratefully acknowledge funding from Fulbright-Hays, the Social Science Research Council, the American Council of Learned Societies, and the American Philosophical Society.

4. See, for example, Barnes; D. Brown; Joseph Murphy; K. Brown; and Thompson. Of these, only Murphy (120–24) discusses syncretism.

5. These conferences have been held in such cities as Ife (Nigeria), Bahia (Brazil), Miami, and New York City. They mark the self-conscious transnationalism of the Òrìṣà tradition, and deserve a special study in this journal.

6. For a sustained and rigorous critique of the rhetoric and ideology of Africanist discourse, see Mudimbe, *The Invention of Africa.*

7. I use the term *syncretic paradigm* to identify the larger model (and its additional concepts) within which the more specific meaning of syncretism proper is located.

8. In "Tolerance," Fernandez recounts Herskovits's affiliation with the NAACP after expressing an initial reluctance (150–51).

9. For a glimpse of the ideological conflict that Herskovits experienced with the Carnegie Corporation, as well as the corporation's colonial epistemology, see Jackson's "Herskovits" (117–18) and "The Making."

10. The "Fon" (also called Dahomeans by Herskovits) and the "Yoruba" are missionary-colonial ethnic designations that emerged in the nineteenth century to refer to peoples of what is today the southern half of the Republic of Benin and southwest Nigeria. The infamous slave port of embarkation was at Ouidah, controlled for a long time by the Portuguese.

11. Thus in Ayede, the Yemoja cult houses the additional deities Orisha Oko, Shango, Ogun, Oshun, Oya, and Olokun.

12. For a more detailed version of this story, see Metraux (42–43).

13. In her discussion of Tshidi Zionists, Jean Comaroff notes how the intent "to deconstruct existing syntagmatic chains, to disrupt paradigmatic associations, and, therefore, to undermine the very coherence of the system they contest" inevitably reproduces, on a formal level, aspects of

the symbolic order which it reconfigures, so that "subversive *bricolages* always perpetuate as they change" (*Body*, 198). It is her association of "syncretistic movements" with subversive bricolages that I am calling "critical practice."

Works Cited

Akinjogbin, I. A. *Dahomey and Its Neighbours, 1708–1818*. Cambridge: Cambridge UP, 1967.

Alonso, Ana M. "Men in 'Rags' and the Devil on the Throne: A Study of Protest and Inversion in the Carnival of Post-Emancipation Trinidad." *Plantation Society in the Americas* 3 (1990): 73–120.

Apter, Andrew. *Black Critics and Kings: The Hermeneutics of Power In Yoruba Society*. Chicago: U of Chicago P, 1992.

Barber, Karin. "How Man Makes God in West Africa: Yoruba Attitudes Toward the *Òrìṣà*." *Africa* 51.3 (1981): 724–45.

Barnes, Sandra T. (ed.) *Africa's Ogun: Old World and New*. Bloomington: Indiana UP, 1989.

Bascom, William. "The Sociological Role of the Yoruba Cult Group." *American Anthropologist* N.S. (46) 1.2 (Memoirs, 63) (1944): 1–75.

Bastide, Roger. *The African Religions of Brazil: Toward a Sociology of Interpenetration of Civilizations*. 1960. Trans. H. Sebba. Baltimore: Johns Hopkins UP, 1978.

Bastien, Rémy. "Vodoun and Politics in Haiti." *Religion and Politics in Haiti*. Ed. H. Courlander and R. Bastien. Washington, DC: Institute for Cross-Cultural Research, 1966.

Brown, David H. "'The Garden in the Machine: Afro-Cuban Sacred Art and Performance in Urban New Jersey and New York." Diss. Yale University, 1989.

Brown, Karen McCarthy. *Mama Lola: A Vodou Priestess in Brooklyn*. Berkeley: U of California P, 1991.

Comaroff, Jean. *Body of Power, Spirit of Resistance: The Culture and History of a South African People*. Chicago: U of Chicago P, 1985.

Comaroff, Jean, and Comaroff, John. *Of Revelation and Revolution: Christianity, Colonialism and Consciousness in South Africa*. Vol. 1. Chicago: U of Chicago P, 1991.

Courlander, H. "Vodoun in Haitian Culture." *Religion and Politics in Haiti*. Ed. H. Courlander and R. Bastien. Washington, DC: Institute for Cross-Cultural Research, 1966.

Curtin, Philip. *The Atlantic Slave Trade: A Census*. Madison: U of Wisconsin P, 1969.

DaMatta, Roberto. *Carnivals, Rogues, and Heroes: An Interpretation of the Brazilian Dilemma*. 1979. Trans. J. Drury. Notre Dame: U of Notre Dame P, 1991.

Davis, Wade. *Passage of Darkness: The Ethnobiology of the Haitian Zombie*. Chapel Hill: U of North Carolina P, 1988.

Derby, Lauren. *Caribbean Nationalism and the Science of Folklore in the Early Twentieth Century*. Unpublished essay, 1992.

Du Bois, W.E.B. *Black Folk, Then and Now: An Essay on the History and Sociology of the Negro Race*. New York: Henry Holt, 1939.

Fernandez, James W. "Tolerance in a Repugnant World and Other Dilemmas in the Cultural Relativism of Melville J. Herskovits." *Ethos* 18.2 (1990): 140–164.

Frazier, E. Franklin. *The Negro Family in the United States*. Chicago: U of Chicago P, 1939.

Freyre, Gilberto. *The Masters and the Slaves: A Study in the Development of Brazilian Civilization*. New York: Knopf, 1956.

Gates, Henry Louis. *The Signifying Monkey: A Theory of Afro-American Literary Criticism*. New York: Oxford UP, 1988.

Herskovits, Melville J. "African Gods and Catholic Saints in New World Negro Belief." *American Anthropologist* ns 39 (1937): 635–43.

———. *The American Negro: A Study of Racial Crossing*. New York: Knopf, 1928.

———. *The Myth of the Negro Past*. Boston: Beacon Press, 1958.

———. *The New World Negro: Selected Papers in Afroamerican Studies*. Bloomington: Indiana UP, 1966.

Hurston, Zora Neale. *Mules and Men*. 1935. Bloomington: Indiana UP, 1978.

———. *Tell My Horse*. Philadelphia: Lippincott, 1938.

Jackson, Walter. "The Making of a Social Science Classic: Gunnar Myrdal's *An American Dilemma*." *Perspectives in American History* 2 (1986): 43–61.

———. "Melville Herskovits and the Search for Afro-American Culture." *Malinowski, Rivers, Benedict and Others: Essays on Culture and Personality*. Ed. George Stocking, Jr. Madison: U of Wisconsin P, 1986. 95–126.

Larose, Serge. "The Meaning of Africa in Haitian Vodu." *Symbols and Sentiments: Cross-Cultural Studies in Symbolism*. Ed. Ioan Lewis. London: Academic, 1977. 85–116.

Law, Robin. *The Oyo Empire, c.1600–c.1836*. Oxford: Clarendon, 1977.

Métraux, Alfred. *Voodoo in Haiti*. 1959. Trans. H. Charteris. New York: Schocken, 1972.

Malinowski, Bronislaw. *Argonauts of the Western Pacific*. 1922. New York: Dutton, 1961.

Mudimbe, Valentin Y. *The Invention of Africa: Gnosis, Philosophy and the Order of Knowledge*. Bloomington: Indiana UP, 1988.

———. "Which Idea of Africa? Herskovits's Cultural Relativism." *October* 55 (1990): 93–104.

Murphy, Joseph. *Santería: An African Religion in America*. Boston: Beacon, 1988.

Ortiz, Fernando. *Hampa Afro-Cubana: Los Negros Esclavos, Estudio de Sociologica y Derecho Publica*. La Habana: Revista Bimestre Cubana, 1916.

Park, Robert E. "The Conflict and Fusion of Cultures with Special Reference to the Negro." *Journal of Negro History* 4 (1919): 111–133.

Parker, Richard G. *Bodies, Pleasures and Passions: Sexual Culture in Contemporary Brazil*. Boston: Beacon, 1991.

Parrinder, E. G. *The Story of Ketu: An Ancient Yoruba Kingdom*. 2nd Edition. Ibadan: Ibadan UP, 1967.

Patterson, Orlando. *Slavery and Social Death: A Comparative Study.* Cambridge: Harvard UP, 1982.

Price, Richard. *First Time: The Historical Vision of an Afro-American People.* Baltimore: Johns Hopkins UP, 1983.

———. *The Guiana Maroons: A Historical and Bibliographic Introduction.* Johns Hopkins UP, 1976.

Price, Sally. *Co-Wives and Calabashes.* Ann Arbor: U of Michigan P, 1984.

Price, Sally, and Richard Price. *Afro-American Arts of the Surinam Rain Forest.* Berkeley: U of California P, 1980.

———. *Two Evenings in Saramaka.* Chicago, U of Chicago P, 1991.

Price-Mars, Jean. *So Spoke the Uncle.* 1928. Trans. M. Shannon. Washington, DC: Three Continents, 1983.

Ramos, Arthur. *As Culturas Negras no Novo Mundo.* Rio de Janeiro, 1937.

Ribeiro, René. *Cultos Afrobrasileiros de Recife: Um Estudo de Ajustemento Social.* Spec. issue of *Boletim do Instituto Joaquim Nabuco.* (1952).

Smith, M. G. "The African Heritage in the Caribbean." *Caribbean Studies: A Symposium.* Ed. Vera Rubin. Jamaica: I.S.E.R., U College of the West Indies, 1957. 34–46.

Thomas, Hugh. *Cuba: The Pursuit of Freedom.* New York: Harper, 1971.

Thompson, Robert F. *Flash of the Spirit: African and Afro-American Art and Philosophy.* New York: Vintage, 1984.

Verger, Pierre F. *Orisha: Les Dieux Yorouba en Afrique et au Nouveau Monde.* Paris: A. M. Metailie, 1982.

Woodson, Carter G. *The African Background Outlined.* Washington, DC: Assoc. for the Study of Negro Life and History, 1936.

That Event, This Memory: Notes on the Anthropology of African Diasporas in the New World

David Scott
Bates College

It was the Atlantic this side of the island, a wild-eyed, marauding sea the color of slate, deep, full of dangerous currents, lined with row upon row of barrier reefs, and with a sound like that of the combined voices of the drowned raised in a loud unceasing lament—all those, the nine million and more it is said, who in their enforced exile, their Diaspora, had gone down between this point and the homeland lying out of sight to the east. This sea mourned them. Aggrieved, outraged, unappeased, it hurled itself upon each of the reefs in turn and then upon the shingle beach, sending up the spume in an angry froth which the wind took and drove in like smoke over the land. Great boulders that had roared down from Westminster centuries ago stood scattered in the surf; these, sculpted into fantastical shapes by the wind and water, might have been gravestones placed there to commemorate those millions of the drowned.

Paule Marshall, *The Chosen Place, the Timeless People*

1. Between Old World and New, Past and Present

In this unforgettable passage, Paule Marshall evokes the relation between the past and the present of the African diaspora, between the historical trauma of an inaugural event and our collective memory of it. In this essay, I am going to concern myself with a certain way of reading this relation, a way that I believe has been a central element in the identity of the anthropology of peoples of African descent in the New World. And a way that, I also believe, is mistaken.

This anthropology has—from its formal inception in the work of Melville J. Herskovits in the late 1920s down to its current elaboration in the work of such contemporary Afro-Americanists and Afro-Caribbeanists as Sidney Mintz and Richard Price—turned in a very profound way around a narrative of "continuities," continuities between the Old World and the New, between the past and the present. The reasons for the privilege and the persistence of such a narrative in the archive of this anthropology are not so hard to come by. After all, it is well enough known that the African presence in the New World began with a sharp and irreversible severance in the holds of slave ships crossing the Middle Passage and in historically unprecedented circumstances of social disordering and social reordering on the colonial slave plantations. Not surprisingly, anthropology manifests a deep, humanist inclination toward a story about continuities and embraces the earnest task of demonstrating the integrity and the intactness of the old in the new, and of the past in the present, of these societies. Nor, likewise, should it be surprising that in the plotting of this narrative of continuities, the two figures of "Africa" and "slavery" have come to form its generative and constitutive points of reference.

Obviously, this story about continuities is not confined within the disciplinary parameters of anthropology. It is a story that has in a variety of ways structured our own "imagined community," our own narratives of identity and tradition. For this reason it would be possible (not to say pertinent) to speak here of at least two historically interconnected yet distinct and analytically separable registers. One is anthropological, strictly speaking, inasmuch as it has to do with the properly disciplinary construction of a distinctive theoretical object, namely, "the New World Negro" (to give it its inaugural name) and the conceptual apparatus employed to identify and represent it. The other is, we might say, extra-anthropological, being transdisciplinary, sometimes positively antidisciplinary, and having rather to do with the varying cultural-political discourses of identity and tradition produced by peoples of African descent in the New World, in the course of our own practices and struggles.[1]

These registers of knowledge-producing cultural practice are of course not identical, but what is noteworthy is that even in nonanthropological discourse, anthropology, taken as the (self-described) "science of culture," is often seen as crucial in providing the authoritative vocabulary in terms of which the claims of difference are established. Anthropology—and for quite definite historical reasons, American cultural anthropology more specifically—has often been taken as providing what we might call the foundational discourse for the cultural politics of identity among peoples of African descent in the New World.[2] Certainly this has been the case at least since Franz Boas's famous commencement address at Atlanta University in 1906 ("The Outlook for the American Negro"), given at the invitation of W. E. B. Du Bois.[3] And it was to become more clearly and more decisively the case with the seminal work of Herskovits two decades later.

I want to inquire here into the specifically disciplinary side of this concern with continuity. I can see that in leaving the "native" texts (so to call them) aside my exercise can only be a partial one. I accept that. But if anthropology, in its capacity as the science of culture, has been able to claim for itself, or have claimed for it, the role of a higher or more foundational authority in the matter of cultural difference, then there is an initial labor of internal, disciplinary interrogation to be carried out, a prior critical accounting for the kind of theoretical object this anthropology establishes and circulates in its authoritative texts on the cultural practices of peoples of African descent in the New World.[4]

First, I shall briefly outline the thesis advanced by one recent contribution to this anthropology, Richard Price's *First-Time: The Historical Vision of an Afro-American People*. In outlining Price's thesis, I will not only emphasize some of the conceptual premises of his argument about a past in which slavery forms the single most important referent but will also inquire into the ideological assumptions of the specifically anthropological problem established through it. To do so will lead me to an inquiry into its links with the inaugural problematic of the "New World Negro" formulated by Herskovits, in whose work it is Africa rather than slavery that forms the single most important referent. I shall seek to argue that in the discursive or narrative economy of this anthropological problematic, *slavery* and *"Africa"* function as virtually interchangeable terms, or, to put it another way, that slavery in the work of Price comes to perform the same rhetorical-conceptual labor as Africa in the work of Herskovits. Both turn on a distinctive attempt to place the "cultures" of the ex-African/ex-slave in relation to what we might call an authentic past, that is, an anthropologically identifiable, ethnologically recoverable, and textually re-presentable past. And what is particularly revealing is that both Price and Herskovits seek to exemplify their arguments about the pasts and cultures of peoples of African descent in the New World on the basis of the study of the same New World peoples, the Saramaka of Suriname.[5]

Though my disagreements will be evident, my reason for adopting the strategy I do is not primarily to criticize either Price or Herskovits. Nor, more importantly, is it my aim to dispense with the trope of continuities as such, or with either (or both) of those profoundly generative and resonant figures—Africa and slavery—through which this description of continuity has been theoretically constructed. As I have already suggested, this pronounced discourse of continuity in the work of Afro-Americanists and Afro-Caribbeanists is in part the measure of the sympathetically affirmative character of the anthropology of peoples of African descent in the New World, the singular mark, one might say, of its strong humanism. My intention, rather, is to indicate what seem to me to be some of the limits of this conception as presently constructed in the authoritative discourse of anthropology; to suggest how inquiring into the formation of conceptual objects such as "the New World Negro" can be of importance in assessing theoretical strategies; and to sketch in something of the outline of an alternative strategy for retaining the concern with continuities in a way theoretically more fruitful to historical and anthropological, or at least to a cultural-critical, inquiry.

2. First-Time

"There was a day in time when the last eyes to see Christ were closed forever." With this arresting and allusive quotation from Jorge Luis Borges as an epigraph, Richard Price, perhaps the leading anthropologist of the Saramaka of the Suriname rain forest, opens his much-acclaimed ethnography, *First-Time: The Historical Vision of an Afro-American People. First-Time* is undoubtedly an ethnography of the first importance. It has indeed, and more than once, been cited as an example of what the best experimentation in contemporary ethnographic writing is all about.[6] Perhaps this is so. Certainly it is true that in this novel work, Price has involved us to an admirable degree in the conditions of the negotiation of his fieldwork, in some of its ethical and epistemological dilemmas. But be that as it may, it is not, strictly speaking, as an exemplary ethnographic text that I shall consider this work of Price's. Or rather, I shall be concerned with the textual strategies it employs only in relation to the substantive argument they support. For to my mind Price's book is important precisely because its textual strategy appears to offer a novel approach to a distinctive anthropological problem, and it is really the seeming nature of this problem that interests me.

Price's opening epigraph is the first and most important clue to the overall structure of his concern: the question of a living collective consciousness of the past in the African diaspora. He writes in the evocative opening lines of this work:

> In a sacred grove beside the river of Dangogo, shaded by equatorial trees, stands a weathered shrine to the Old-Time People (*Amonenge*), those ancestors who "heard the guns of war." Whenever there is a collective crisis in the region—should the rains refuse to come on time or an epidemic sweep the river—it is to this shrine that Saramakas repair. As libations of sugarcane beer moisten the earth beneath the newly raised flags, the Old-Time People are one by one invoked—their names spoken (or played on the *apinti* drum), their deeds recounted, their foibles recalled, and the drums/dances/songs that they once loved performed to give them special pleasure. (5)

The Saramaka, a New World people today numbering roughly twenty thousand, are descendants of Africans sold into slavery in Dutch Guiana (today's Suriname) in the late seventeenth and early eighteenth centuries. These ancestors, however, the "Old-Time People," escaped into the forested hinterland and established there "maroon"[7] communities fiercely independent of the coastal colonial slave plantation system (see Price, *The Guiana Maroons* and *To Slay the Hydra*). And they, along with neighboring maroon communities such as the Djuka, the Aluku, and the Kwinti, have to this day remained a distinct and more or less precariously autonomous people. If the story of the coming of Africans to the New World—their capture, their deracination, their enslavement—is told as tragedy (as among modern historians it most often is), then its most compelling heroes are these maroons.[8] Theirs must be the most remarkable instance of sustained collective resistance in the history of New World colonial slavery. African slaves escaping the clutches of the colonial plantation early enough to avoid European cultural influence, and in large enough numbers to establish independent communities in the new soil of the Americas: no other New World people seem more to exemplify the moment of transit between the Old World and the New, between the past and the present.

Price opens his argument in *First-Time* with the statement of what he takes to be an essential conceptual paradox: whereas thousands of individual Saramakas, he says, must actually have "heard the guns of war," that is, must actually have lived during the time of the colonial war against the Saramakas (between the 1680s and the Peace of 1762), the names of only a small fraction of these ancestors are today invoked at the shrine to the Old-Time People. Therefore, Price maintains, history (by which he means the "consciousness" of a specifiable past) is clearly "selective." And the uniqueness of *First-Time,* he suggests,

> lies in its taking seriously the selection that is made by those people who gather at this shrine. It is about those people and those long-ago events that Saramakas today choose to think about, talk about and act upon; but it is also about the ways that Saramakas transform the general past (everything that happened) into the significant past, their history. This book is an attempt to communicate something of the Saramakas' own special vision of their formative years.

And Price does, with consummate care and an evident ethnographic generosity, communicate to us something of this special vision of the Saramaka. As we read of the legendary Fankia who "heard the guns of war" and who conveyed to her people how they should henceforth speak with the Old Time People, we feel the force of a profound and demanding past and see how, for the Saramaka, Fankia instantiates an inaugural site of historical authority. But as we shall see, Price's book is actually more than this attempt to convey to us the flavor of the historical vision of the Saramaka. In fact, it attempts to corroborate that vision, to put before us evidence from contemporary colonial sources that are supposed to confirm that the events of which his Saramaka informants speak were an historical actuality, that they really happened. Indeed it is the slippage between this desire on the one hand to share with us the "special vision" of the Saramakas and the desire on the other to confirm the historical truth of what the Saramaka tell that forms the central tension of *First-Time,* and this makes it an exemplary instance of that kind of (I think unsatisfactory) anthropological problematic that sees its task as one of representing authentic pasts.

First-time knowledge, knowledge, that is, of that inaugural era of struggle against the Dutch colonial army, is crucial to Saramaka culture and collective identity. It is knowledge that marks out for them a temporal and even a spatial break, a threshold of exile and slavery beyond which they passed only with the most sustained sacrifice, and that must now be held up for generations to come as a constant danger, the ever-present possibility of a return that must, at all costs, be prevented.[9] As a result, first-time knowledge is distinguished, for example, from knowledge of the more recent past by what Price calls "its overwhelming inherent power" (*First-Time* 6). And for this reason it is an area of local knowledge that is "singularly circumscribed, restricted, and guarded" (6). It is a knowledge that, as Price informs us, requires special handling (because such knowledge, Saramaka people say, can "kill"); special occasions of utterance (e.g., "cock's crow," the hour or two just before dawn); and specialist keepers (individual Saramakas who, for one reason or another, become renowned as repositories of Saramaka historical knowledge).

Moreover, first-time knowledge is knowledge that requires special discursive forms of utterance. Interestingly, the Saramaka have no Great Narrative of their origins, the kind of single, interconnected story that, passing through discernible and successive phases of beginning, middle, and end, brings us from that day to this. Rather, first-time knowledge is embedded in a variety of other, disparate sorts of discursive or rhetorical forms: as Price describes them, they include "genealogical nuggets," personal epithets, commemorative place-names, proverbs, songs, etc. And this knowledge is preeminently a knowledge of "events." For Saramakas, Price maintains, it is the "event" that constitutes the "very stuff of history." He writes:

> In the present book, my unit of analysis is the event. Taking fragments (often a mere phrase) from many different men, comparing them, discussing them with others, challenging them against rival accounts, and eventually holding them up

against contemporary written evidence, I try to develop a picture of what the most knowledgeable Saramakas know, and why they know and preserve it. (*First-Time* 25)

Now in the development of this "picture of what the most knowledgeable Saramakas know," Price adopts a unique and compelling strategy of ethnographic representation. The substantive portion of the text of *First-Time* is divided into two parts occupying the upper and lower halves of each page, running like simultaneous "channels" of narrative. In the upper channel, we read Saramaka accounts of a specific "event"; in the lower, a commentary on these events. These commentaries, Price maintains, are intended to serve at least three functions. The first two—regarding the intelligibility of the accounts to those uninitiated in Saramaka discourse and the special meaning each has for the individual Saramaka informant uttering it—are fairly straightforward and need not concern us here. The third function, however, is conceptually the most interesting and indeed the most crucial for the point of Price's argument: it serves to introduce "information from contemporary written sources—chronology, geography, and other facts" in order to "work toward a picture of 'what really happened' against which we can measure and grasp the complex processes of selection used by Saramakas in regard to their distant past" (*First-Time* 39).

Such, briefly sketched, is the bold and innovative ethnographic strategy of *First-Time*. It tells a powerful story about continuities between the present and a past called slavery. I shall suggest, however, that it is really only a plausible strategy insofar as we accept the conceptual premise (i.e., that pasts are preservable and representable) and the ideological assumption (i.e., that the special task of an anthropology of peoples of the African diaspora consists in providing the apparatus for corroborating pasts) that organize the theoretical object it seeks to elaborate.

There is in Price's argument a notable ambiguity that turns on what one might call the agenda of historical understanding, on what is believed to be at stake in understanding a people's consciousness of its past. Price tells us that Saramaka discourse about their past, about plantation slavery and their struggle against it, is a "selective" one and that what is selected is of significance to the structure of expectations operating in the present. However, this selective, constructed past is not so much examined to reveal the reasons for particular selections as to show the verifiable actuality of the content of Saramaka statements about it. For Price, the really important problem thrown up by the selective character of Saramaka discourse about the past is not the economy of significance in which selections operate. Though Price does indicate the ideological character of first-time knowledge, he does not do so by way of opening access to a formal discussion in this register. Referential accuracy is his principal concern, so the anthropological problem that presents itself to us is not, as it might have been, that of mapping or describing the ways in which the past is ideologically produced and used by the Saramaka in the construction of authoritative cultural traditions and distinctive identities, the variable ways these constructions are negotiated, become conventions, are subverted, are redescribed, and so on, but rather that of determining how far what is selected actually happened, how far it is indeed an accurate representation of what really was.

Such a conceptual strategy must then logically presuppose the availability of an historical/interpretive apparatus that can identify and represent "what really happened" in the Saramaka past, independent of Saramaka accounts of it; it must do so in order to provide historical representations that can be employed as a sort of authoritative baseline against which to measure the accuracy of their own memory of it. In Price's text this historical apparatus consists of the archive of Dutch colonial documents about the period in question. This archive, it follows, is not so much to be "read," that is, to be interrogated as a discursive density, an irreducible configuration of colonial politics and ideological textualization, but to verify Saramaka statements about certain events. To point this out is not to impugn the use of archival material in anthropological research but rather to differ with what appears to be Price's view, namely, that both the oral testimony of his Saramaka informants and the written texts of the Dutch colonizers are culturally different, yet conceptually uncomplicated, ways of re-presenting the past in the present.[10]

Price's conception of historical consciousness, then, is not a very coherent one. However, the epistemological issues of how to adequately know the Saramaka past and what kind of evidence would serve to substantiate it are less intrinsically interesting to me here than the question of the ideological assumptions that serve to secure the seeming authority of such anthropological arguments regarding it. In my reading, this is where the important stakes lie. And these ideological assumptions have to do with the kind of anthropological object that the Afro-American or the Afro-Caribbean (or anyway the New World Negro) has historically been constructed as. I would argue that at least one of the pervasive ideological assumptions through which this theoretical object has been constructed is that peoples of African descent in the New World require something like anthropology, a science of culture, to provide them with the foundational guarantee of an authentic past.

Price wants to demonstrate conclusively that an Afro-American people does indeed have an accurate memory of past events. But why, we might ask, does this need to be demonstrated in the first place? What are the ideological conditions that motivate it? Or, to put it another way: What are the sources that give special significance to the bold subtitle of Price's ethnography—"the historical vision of an Afro-American People"? For what is implicit in its inclusive claim is that this "historical vision" of the Saramaka that is about to be described to us, is, in some way, to be taken as illustrative of the historical vision of Afro-American people as such. The Saramaka, in short, are a sort of anthropological metonym; they are to be understood as providing the exemplary arena in which to argue out certain anthropological claims about a discursive domain called Afro-America. And here, I think, is the first thing to notice about the ideological structure of *First-Time:* its place within the genealogy of a specific anthropological problem, that is, the problem of the African in the New World.

First-Time is a compelling piece of ethnography, in part because it seems a nearly conclusive rebuttal of that old anthropological notion regarding the supposed "timelessness" of primitive peoples, their lack of "historical consciousness." *First-Time,* like Renato Rosaldo's *Ilongot Headhunting,* presents the case that this is nothing but an anthropological (or, if you like, western) prejudice; Price more or less explicitly says so.[11] I suggest, however, that much of the seeming power of Price's argument derives from another source, that is, its more local agenda, its concern to put to rest the prominent notion that peoples of African descent in the New World suffer from "pastlessness."[12] Curiously enough, while explicit expression of this agenda is suppressed in the body of *First-Time* itself, it becomes the subject of a small, almost unnoticed essay on "Caribbean historical consciousness"[13] published soon after. In this essay, Price takes as his target what he calls the "denial of history" to the New World descendants of Africans—the "vanguard for those people to whom history has too often been denied" ("An Absence of Ruins?" 24). A number of West Indian writers—most notably, V. S. Naipaul, Orlando Patterson, and Derek Walcott—are singled out for sharp criticism. These writers, in Price's estimate of them, are complicit in the argument (a "bourgeois illusion, a function of our [?] own ethnocentrism") that "Caribbean peoples suffer from a profound lack of historical consciousness, that they know (and care) almost nothing about their own complex and often unhappy pasts" (25). And a bit later he tells us, "[t]he strongest evidence I could muster against the notion of a pastless Afro-Caribbean is undoubtedly contained in *First-Time.* That book lays bare a vision of the past with overwhelming relevance to present-day Saramakas" (27).

I do not want to enter here into the interesting question of Price's reading (or misreading, as I think it is) of the historical imaginary of West Indian literature. That I will leave to others.[14] My concern is only to indicate something of the ideological location of *First-Time*. On the basis of the verification of an authentic consciousness of a past in which slavery forms the generative referential moment, it sets itself against the pervasive assumption of the "pastlessness" of peoples of African descent in the New World. The Saramaka—uniquely situated as they are—are the exemplary stage upon which both this problem of the pasts of Afro-American diasporas and its anthropological resolution can be set out in sharpest relief. The following question then poses itself: What are the historical sources of this idea that the theoretical problem posed by the existence of peoples of African descent in the New World consists in corroborating their past? I want now to turn my attention to this.

3. The Anthropological Problem of "the New World Negro"

The anthropological problem of peoples of African descent in the New World is more a problem constituted by American cultural anthropology than by British social anthropology, and it bears the distinctive marks of that determinate origin. If British social anthropology has been criticized (often justly) for its relation to the British Empire and to the sources, structures, and representations of colonial rule, American cultural anthropology has had the good fortune to appear in a much less unsavory light. Perhaps with reason. For Franz Boas (the leading figure in the founding of professional American anthropology) not only opened the way for a concept of "culture" according to which each people's practices were to be taken on their own terms but was himself an outspoken critic of racial and ethnic discrimination (see Boas, "Outlook"; Stocking, "Anthropology"; and Hyatt). This distinction, however, should not obscure the necessity of inquiring into the ideological determinants of the discourse of American cultural anthropology. The question to be addressed here is not the often-repeated (if nevertheless important) one regarding the dearth of adequate anthropological research on Afro-American culture (see Willis; Szwed) but rather that of how the object itself, Afro-America, came to be constituted in the texts of this cultural discourse.

Richard Price is not the first American anthropologist to study the Saramaka. Nor is he the first to envision that the Saramaka offer, in some way, the key to the anthropological problem of the African in the New World. He is preceded on both counts by Melville J. Herskovits.[15] A student of Franz Boas (and much influenced by him in this regard) Herskovits, perhaps more than anyone, helped to establish the "New World Negro" as a positive anthropological problem, that is to say, as a visible and distinctive problem of "history" and "culture."[16]

Herskovits's contribution to the formation of an anthropology of the "New World Negro" is inseparable from two other debates. One is the wider discourse that constructed the Negro as a *social* problem of a certain kind, and the other is that discussion of the conceptual categories of the nascent "science of culture" that formulated the New World Negro as a *theoretical* problem of a certain kind. Though it is impossible to delineate here the full historical complexity of these social and ideological preconditions, it is necessary to point to at least some aspects that were crucial to the conceptual problematic into which Herskovits inserted himself.

In its social and ideological aspects, the "Negro Question" in the pre–First World War years of this century had to do with whether the Negro could be considered a candidate for full social and moral citizenship in the American body-politic.[17] Could the Negro become assimilated to the values and ethos of American society? Or was there something distinctive about the Negro that either precluded, or at any rate seriously qualified, assimilation? In one way or another, this question of the Negro's ambiguous identity turned on the idea, pervasive at the turn of the century, that Negroes were a people with no consequential past and therefore a people with no distinctive contribution to Civilization, no Culture in the Arnoldian sense. This idea was itself linked to two other images: the image of slavery as an institution that had completely erased the African identities of the slaves and the image of Africa as itself a dark and savage place (see Fredrickson). Framed as it was by an evolutionary tradition presided over by Herbert Spencer (Stocking, "Franz Boas"), much of the social-science thinking of this period accepted these assumptions and images. Certainly these questions formed part of the ideological atmosphere in which the professional discipline of modern American anthropology emerged; indeed it could be said that these questions were part of the ideological horizon on which the new anthropology defined itself and the distinctive labor of its seminal concept: culture.

Between the late 1880s and the turn of the century, Boas had set about what we might call a strategy of skeptical interrogation (see Krupat) of the two existing "branches" of anthropology, the "biological" and the "psychological." In so doing, he demonstrated the unpersuasiveness of their arguments (regarding, on the one hand, the question of the mental ability of different races and, on the other, the historical reconstruction of the stages of the social development of "mankind"), as well as the ideological overdetermination of their claims for the superiority of the West. This skeptical interrogation would have a number of strong conceptual effects: among them, the displacement of "race" as the explanatory key to difference; the antihierarchical revaluation of this difference as "culture"; and the reconfiguring of the "science" of anthropology around the historical and ethnographic study of particular, that is, "cultural," instances of difference.

Most pertinent to our concern with the conceptual preconditions of the anthropology of "the New World Negro," these cultural instances, Boas argued, have to be analytically understood in terms of the psychological and historical integration of "elements" into "wholes." Cultures are distinctive (and therefore valid) by virtue of the growth of an inner unity (a "style" or "ethos") composed of traits transmitted or diffused historically from place to place or group to group. The culture of any tribe, Boas maintained, "no matter how primitive it may be, can be fully explained only when we take into consideration its inner growth as well as its relation to the culture of its near and distant neighbors and the effect that they may have exerted" ("Principles" 278). Not only were all cultures valid—the European no more than the African—but they each bore a distinctive relation to the pasts from which they were derived. In view of this (for its time) quite radical reformulation of the question of difference, it is not surprising that Boas responded to the contemporary racist image of black culture by attempting to place it in a certain proximity to an anthropologically rehabilitated representation of its African past. For it followed from Boas's conception of "cultural" difference that any appreciation of Afro-America would have to consider "its relation to the culture of its near and distant neighbors." This is, in fact, what Boas attempted to demonstrate at Atlanta University in 1906 when he "reminded" his audience of black graduates of the past cultural "achievements" of their African forebears ("Outlook").

What is most notable about Boas's remarks about black culture, however, is not only their authoritative force, but the fact that they stopped short of claiming any essential "Africanness" for Afro-American culture. For Boas, the culture of "the New World Negro" is not set in a direct, continuous relation to the ethnohistorical African past he authoritatively evokes. The "genius" or geist of Afro-Americans, that feature which gave to their varied practices the "wholeness" or "integrity" that Boas claimed for "culture," is not traced in some (analytically salient) way to this evoked Africa. Rather, this ethnologically rehabilitated Africa supports a past that belongs to the Negro only as a potential source of inspiration, something toward which such young Afro-American intellectuals as Boas was himself addressing in Atlanta might confidently cast a nostalgic backward glance even as they tackled the hard (and as Boas no doubt believed, real) work of racial uplift. This attitude reflects perhaps the cautious, assimilationist tenor of cultivated politics, both white and black, in liberal America in the prewar years—the confidence in "the marvelous power of amalgamation of our nation," as Boas ("Principles" 202) put it. For it was indeed a politically delicate issue; to have asserted the distinctiveness of Afro-Americans at a time when difference was still argued out in racial terms would have provided grist for the mill of racist segregationists, for whom blacks were so different as to be unassimilable. Yet Boas's ethnological evocation of Africa was in its way a profoundly significant moment, and it is not hard to see the cause of Du Bois's enthusiasm; for here, in the white anthropologist's statement, was the enigmatic sign of our racial memory, the metaphorical Ethiopia and Egypt of the recently published *Souls of Black Folk* ("The shadow of a mighty Negro past flits through the tale of Ethiopia the Shadowy and of Egypt the Sphinx" [3]), given a tangible, that is to say, a scientific grounding and guarantee.

The conditions of the relation between Boasian "culture" and Afro-America changed considerably after the First World War, so that anthropology would more precisely specify this illusive grounding (i.e., Africa) and so address more boldly, more declaratively, the question of the scientific guarantee of Afro-American race-pride. There were at least two kinds of reasons for this change, one having to do with conditions of race ideology that saw the advent of a "new" Negro (see Locke) and the other with developments in what George Stocking (*Ethnographic Sensibility* 210) has referred to as the "classic" period of modern American anthropology.

Over the course of the war years, the political conditions of race ideology (as indeed of much else about the texture of social life in the United States) altered so that "talented tenth" assimilationism was increasingly brought into question by a more vigorous, more uncompromising cultural nationalism (Huggins, *Voices*). One consequence of this was that across a range of contemporary Afro-American ideological positions—from the working-class disciples of Marcus Garvey to the intellectual organizers of Pan-Africanism and the artists and literati of the Harlem Renaissance—peoples of African descent were themselves reclaiming, in various inflections, a past called Africa, and placing it in the foreground of their assertions of cultural identity and community.[18] I think something of this widespread mood is heard in the Harlem essayist and bibliophile Arthur Schomburg's contribution to Alain Locke's *The New Negro*. Schomburg, who opens his remarkable essay, "The Negro Digs Up his Past," by suggesting that Afro-Americans could not embrace the Emersonian idea that in America it "is unnecessary to have a past," closes with the rousing assertion that though the Negro has been maligned as "a man without a history because he has been considered a man without a worthy culture," he was now seeing "himself against a reclaimed background, in a perspective that will give pride and self-respect ample scope, and make history yield for him the same values that the treasured past of any people affords" (Schomburg 237). And yet, at least by that very measure which the well-informed Schomburg himself invoked—the evidence of African ethnology—this background was still vague, undefined. As the late Nathan Huggins put it in his brilliant discussion of the cultural politics of 1920s Harlem: "All seemed to know, or sense, that Africa should mean something to the race; there should be some race memory that tied black men together; [however,] ambiguity and doubt always left the question unresolved" (*Harlem Renaissance* 80–81).

The ideological space into which Melville Herskovits entered, having taken his degree with Boas at Columbia University in 1923, was characterized by a complex of positions in which the past and its signal figure, Africa, played a critical role in articulating a positive relation to being somehow both distinctively Negro and American. Certainly in these altered ideological circumstances, the question "How could Afro-American race-pride be placed on a scientific footing?" must have appeared to a Boas-trained student like Herskovits (who himself had many prominent friends in the Harlem community[19]) to demand a different, or at least a less equivocal, answer than the one given it by Boas two decades before. And certainly, too, the discipline's emerging scientific self-consciousness in these years made such an answer seem possible.

For by the middle 1920s the professionalization of American anthropology had begun to lend to its practitioners an air of intellectual confidence and scientific authority. After all, the discipline could now boast its own "laboratory"[20] (as was powerfully demonstrated by Margaret Mead's South Seas research), and, in the various approaches of Mead, Ruth Benedict, and Robert Redfield, it employed an increasingly streamlined and sophisticated methodological apparatus. However, the development during this period that is particularly pertinent to our concern with the formation of an anthropology of the New World Negro is the elaboration of the concept of "acculturation." Adumbrated in Boas's idea of the historical dissemination and integration of cultural elements,[21] acculturation by the late 1920s and early 1930s was acquiring a conceptual distinctiveness and scholarly appeal. As programmatically outlined by Redfield, Ralph Linton, and Herskovits in their memorandum for the Social Science Research Council, the concept was sharply distinguished from such other related concepts in the Boasian lexicon as "culture-change," "assimilation," and "diffusion"; it was given a definitional precision and methodological rigor that it was lacking hitherto. The study of acculturation was to be oriented around the careful identification of "traits," and the problem of their selection, their determination, and their integration into other patterns. This identification and classification of traits was further to be combined with an investigation of the "psychological mechanisms" of selection and integration.

This view retained the inaugural Boasian idea of culture as constituted of essential, quantifiable elements or units integrated into a psychologically meaningful whole that was unproblematically representable in ethnographic texts. It also added to that base a more positivist program of inquiry: a methodological apparatus for systematically identifying and classifying these traits, for tracing their authentic origins and sources, and for conceptualizing the way they fit into an essential cultural totality. So conceived, the anthropology of acculturation was scientifically more credible. Moreover, if Boasian anthropology still retained (as indeed it did in an even more urgent way than before the war) the socially conscious conviction that its science could have the practical humanist effect of inspiring Afro-Americans with race-pride, this could now arguably be accomplished in less speculative, more empirically sound terms. Herskovits's seminal contribution to the anthropology of the New World Negro, I suggest, may be read as an attempt to demonstrate how the Negro could indeed be both distinctively Negro and American, and to do so in the context of a new, more assured, science of culture (see Jackson).

In the early 1920s, Herskovits still held the assimilationist view, common enough among white American liberals, that the Negro was not culturally distinct, but was indeed as American as anyone else: "the same pattern, only a different shade!" as he famously put it in his contribution to *The New Negro* ("The Negro's Americanism" 353). Even as late as 1927 he could speak of Afro-Americans as a people "of the most diverse racial stock, yet living the life of white Americans" ("Acculturation" 224). But by the end of this momentous decade of black cultural expression, Herskovits, deeply influenced by the vocal and assertive wave of black consciousness, completely reversed this position, and began to outline the ideas he would become best known for.[22] On the basis of a number of ethnographic studies (of which *Life in a Haitian Valley* [1937] is perhaps the best loved), and works of conceptual refiguration (of which *The Myth of the Negro Past* [1941] is doubtless the best known), which together constitute the cornerstone of an anthropology of African diasporas in the New World, Herskovits set out to demonstrate that not only was the New World Negro culturally distinct, but that this distinctiveness was owed precisely to an authentic African heritage.

Significantly, the first place to which Herskovits went in this undertaking to uncover the distinctive Africanness of Afro-American culture was to the then Dutch colony of Suriname, visiting (with his wife, Frances) in the summers of 1928 and 1929. Sketching retrospectively the path of their successive concerns as they wrote *Rebel Destiny: Among the Bush Negroes of Dutch*

Guiana, their popular description of 1920s Saramaka life, the Herskovitses wrote:

> It began in 1923 with the inquiry into Negro-white crossing in the United States. As this work progressed it became evident that the problem demanded more knowledge of the sources of the slaves who compose the Negro ancestry of the American Negroes than was available. This knowledge, which historical documents do not give us, was, therefore, to be sought in a comparison of Negro cultures in the New World and Africa. (viii–ix)

On this conception—one in which an understanding of contemporary cultural practice requires a knowledge of its authentic sources—the North American Negro (in terms of whom the problem as such was formulated) remained something of an enigma. It therefore became necessary, or so it seemed, to go elsewhere in search of the sources of the North American Negro. Already in the early 1930s, then, Herskovits was constructing the metonymic narrative that would join Afro-America into a whole differentiated by a measurable proximity to Africa.

In their study of Dutch Suriname, the Herskovitses adopted the comparative strategy of studying both the Saramaka of the hinterland and the town Surinamese of Paranaraibo, the capital. Their assumptions are obvious. The Surinamese of the town, by virtue of their long association with European culture, were less likely to have retained as many of the traits of Africa as the Saramaka in the "bush." And indeed the Herskovitses found that the critical difference between the bush and the town is that "the bush is Africa of the seventeenth century" (x). Putting it more sharply, they write:

> The importance of the Bush Negroes for the student of Negro cultures, then, is that they live and think today as did their ancestors who established themselves in this bush, which is to say that they live and think much as did the Negroes who were brought to other parts of the New World, and who became the ancestors of the New World Negroes of the present day. (xii)

By 1930, soon after Herskovits's return from Suriname, he elaborated what he called a "scale of intensity of Africanisms," on the basis of which he argued the possibility of measuring the degree and the extent to which the Negro in the New World had actually retained elements of African culture.

> It is quite possible on the basis of our present knowledge to make a kind of chart indicating the extent to which the descen-

dants of Africans brought to the New World have retained Africanisms in their cultural behavior. If we consider the intensity of African cultural elements in the various regions north of Brazil . . . we may say that after Africa itself it is the Bush Negroes of Suriname who exhibit a civilization which is the most African. . . . Next to them, on our scale, would be placed their Negro neighbors on the coastal plains of the Guianas, who, in spite of centuries of close association with the whites, have retained an amazing amount of their aboriginal African traditions, many of which are combined in curious fashion with the traditions of the dominant group. (149)

And so on, until: "Finally, we should come to a group where, to all intents and purposes, there is nothing of the African tradition left, and which consists of people of varying degrees of Negroid physical type, who only differ from their white neighbors in the fact that they have more pigmentation in their skins" (150). From the Bush Negroes of Suriname at one end of the "scale of intensity of Africanisms" to North American blacks at the other, Herskovits was reconstructing the precise extent to which the New World Negro had retained the Old in the New, the past in the present.

This, I think it is fair to say, is the inaugural moment of a lasting anthropological problematic. The New World Negro had been ideologically constituted by a dominant and racist nineteenth century discourse as a figure with neither a determinate past nor, its supposed corollary, a distinctive culture. And by the mid-1920s, black counterdiscourses were, in the articulation of a radical identity-politics, making impressive and unignorable claims for an active African heritage. Therefore, on the conceptual terrain established by the categories of Boasian culture, the task presented to the new anthropology was to show in as scientifically conclusive a way as possible that the New World Negro did in fact have both a determinate past and a distinctive culture. Since Africa was assumed to be the authentic cultural origin of the Negro diaspora, Herskovits set out to demonstrate, by an effort of corroboration, the remnants of that past in the cultural traits of contemporary Negro societies. The Saramaka, then, seemed to provide the unique possibility of demonstrating this.

Richard Price, it is true, is not concerned with cultural retentions as such. He is not trying to show that there are authentic traits of a past called Africa still around in the New World.[23] The anthropological conception of culture had in the meantime drifted away from the hard, positivist ground of traits towards the more semiotic field of symbols and "consciousness,"[24] and ideological conditions after the 1960s no longer required (or at least not in the same way as in the early decades of this century) that the New World Negro be placed in direct proximity to a rehabilitated figure of Africa. Rather, Price wants to show that there is an authentic "memory" or "consciousness" of a past called slavery. But it is not hard to see that in spite of this apparent difference, both Herskovits and Price share a fundamental assumption regarding the history and culture of peoples of African descent in the New World, namely, that their history and culture has to be anthropologically argued out in terms of a notion of an authentic past (whatever its name, whatever its modality) persisting in the present and that this persisting past, moreover, can be conclusively demonstrated on the ethnographic example of an exemplary case, the Saramaka of Suriname, a people supposedly closest in proximity to that past.

4. Between That Event and This Memory: Tradition

I would like to propose that we attempt to change this anthropological problematic altogether, this sustained preoccupation with the corroboration or verification of authentic pasts. The issue has nothing to do with erasing either of the figures of Africa or slavery (or even the resonant narrative of continuity that embodies them) from the anthropology of peoples of African descent in the New World. Rather, what I propose is their theoretical relocation; between that event (Africa or slavery) and this memory there spreads a complex discursive field we may usefully call "tradition."[25] By tradition I have in mind a differentiated field of discourse whose unity, such as it is, resides not in anthropologically authenticated traces, but in its being constructed around a distinctive group of tropes or figures, which together perform quite specific kinds of rhetorical labor.

The first and most obvious of tradition's labors is to secure connections among a past, a present, and a future. In the theoretical field occupied by the work of Herskovits and Price, the figures of Africa and slavery circulate as authentic presences, which anthropology is supposed to make legible in the practices or consciousnesses of the descendants of Africans and slaves. The project I commend would be concerned with the following kinds of questions: What are the varying ways in which Africa and slavery are employed by New World peoples of African descent in the narrative construction of relations among pasts, presents, and futures? What, in each case, are the salient features with which these figures are inscribed? What is the rhetorical or, if you like, ideological, work that they are made to perform in the varied instances and occasions in which they are brought into play? For example, the "first-time" of Rastafarians in Jamaica (and Rastafarians do speak of "first-time"), like that of the Saramakas, turns on the central figure of slavery; but it is likely to be inscribed with a different set of ideological investments, reflecting its own specific historical and political conditions. What would be at stake here is less whether one can measure the extent to which this disaporan community of Rastafarians retains an accurate memory of any verifiable preemancipation event than the ways in which this figure, slavery (and those figures metaphorically and metonymically connected to it), enables (or prevents) establishment of positions in a cultural and political field.

Cultural traditions, however, are not only authored; they are authorized. They not only make intelligible; they make legitimate. The second of tradition's labors therefore has to do with securing what we might call a distinctive community of adherents. What space do Africa and slavery occupy in the political economy of local discourse? To what kinds of authority do they make their appeal? From what kinds of audience do they seek their support? What are the conditions—discursive and nondiscursive—of reception that facilitate their persuasiveness? Take, for example, the uses of the figure of Africa by Arthur Schomburg (the bibliophile) and Marcus Garvey (the mass leader), or again, its uses in the verses of a Calypsonian, on the one hand, and the political rhetoric of a Michael Manley, on the other. The point is that this figure can have different political uses, different modes of authorization, can address itself to a variety of audiences—and yet at the same time belong to a distinctive tradition insofar as a single figure is being employed in the construction of a relation between pasts and presents.

The third of tradition's labors is to link narratives of the past to narratives of identity. This is of course because tradition seeks not only to make the past intelligible and legitimate but also to instruct, that is to say, to actively cultivate the virtues it valorizes. How are the figures of Africa and Slavery employed in the fashioning of specific virtues, in the cultivation of specific dispositions, specific modes of address, specific styles—of dress, of speech, of song, of the body's movements; how, in other words, do these figures participate in those techniques by means of which the construction of appropriate bodies and selves are effected?

It seems to me that these kinds of questions enable us to ask theoretically more interesting questions about pasts in the present. It might be noted too that they are not, on the one hand, essentialist, inasmuch as they do not presuppose the full or partial presence of an Africa or slavery that needs only to pass through the interpretive grid of anthropology to be recognized and appreciated as such. Nor, on the other hand, are they antiessentialist, inasmuch as they do not assert that there is no actual continuity between Africa or slavery and the present, that these are merely empty signifiers. These questions in fact do not seek to make any claims whatsoever regarding the ultimate ontological status of Africa and slavery in the present of the cultures of the New World and therefore do not see the theoretical task of anthropological inquiry as trying either to accurately represent the proximity between the present and the past or to deny it. At the same time, these questions affirm that peoples of African descent in the New World do make of Africa and slavery a profound presence in their cultural worlds, and seek rather to describe the tradition of discourse in which they participate, the local network of power and knowledge in which they are employed, and the kinds of identities they serve to fashion.

Notes

Versions of this paper have been read at the University of California, Santa Cruz; Northeastern University, Boston; and Rice University, Houston. I have benefited from the comments offered on each of these occasions. I am especially grateful to Elizabeth Eames for her searching criticism of an earlier draft and to Herman Gray, in conversations with whom many of the ideas expressed here were discussed.

1. These, of course, may be either popular or scholarly, but this distinction may be bracketed for my purposes in this essay.

2. There is a contemporary story, in many ways a counterhegemonic story, according to which anthropology is central to undoing the hegemonic master narrative of the West. In this story, anthropology, as the discourse of culture, is counterposed to Philosophy, the adjudicative discourse of Reason. It is thus seen as a potential way of empowering Other rationalities—i.e., culture(s)—against Reason (or at least, Reason as a distinctive kind of cultural knowledge, that of the West since the Enlightenment). But it is perhaps not sufficiently appreciated how in so doing "culture" itself can be made to simply replace Reason as new authentic foundation, the ground, so to put it, for another ontology.

3. The text of this lecture is reproduced in Boas ("Outlook"). Its effect on the young Du Bois is now well known. In a famous passage in the preface to his *Black Folk, Then and Now* (1939), he wrote: "Franz Boas came to Atlanta University where I was teaching history in 1906 and said to a graduating class: You need not be ashamed of your African past; and then he recounted the history of the black kingdoms south of the Sahara for a thousand years. I was too astonished to speak. All of this I had never heard and I came then and afterwards to realize how . . . silence and neglect . . . can let truth utterly disappear or . . . be unconsciously distorted" (vii).

4. The distinction is, I think, an important one to insist on. For note that what anthropology constructs is a theoretical object, not a cultural identity (except insofar as anthropology has now become crucial to the cultural identity of the West [see McGrane]). Another possible task might be to inquire into the ways in which the anthropological object gets appropriated by peoples of African descent in the New World for their various purposes.

5. In a recent comment on anthropological theory, Arjun Appadurai has made the instructive point that anthropology has not sufficiently problematized the relation between place and theory (356–61). This is a point I wish both to endorse and elaborate.

6. In the course of a discussion of the possible ways open to a postmodernist anthropology, James Clifford has written of *First-Time* that it "is evidence of the fact that acute political and epistemological self-consciousness need not lead to ethnographic self-absorption, or to the conclusion that it is impossible to know anything certain about other people" (7). See also Marcus and Fischer.

7. "The English word *maroon*," writes Price (in one of the unpaginated pages), "derived from the Spanish *cimarron*, a term originally used in Hispaniola to refer to domestic cattle that had taken

to the hills; by the early 1500s, it had come to be used in plantation colonies throughout the Americas to designate slaves who successfully escaped from captivity."

8. For a discussion of the tropic emplotment of historical reconstruction, see White.

9. This is like "the time of the Japanese" of the Ilongot of the Philippines studied by Rosaldo in "Doing Oral History" and *Ilongot Headhunting*. Rosaldo, in a more nuanced and theoretically self-reflexive way, shares some of the same faulty concepts.

10. It is part of Price's concern to caution us against the uncritical imposition of Western assumptions about history (supposedly the idea of history as, quintessentially, written documents) and to encourage us to a closer and more careful attention to the distinctive local (and very often oral) ways of re-presenting the past in the present. Notwithstanding the fact that the idea that the authorized version of the past is the written one is not in itself a western idea (witness for example the Sinhalas' conception of their Great Chronicle, the *Mahavamsa*), this doubt is a worthy one and the advice useful.

11. Note the epigraphs taken from Robert H. Lowie and A. R. Radcliffe-Brown that open the second chapter, "Of Speakers/To Readers."

12. Part of the problem with Price's argument is that there is a conflation of these two related but distinguishable registers, "timelessness" and "pastlessness." "Timelessness" has to do with the primitive's supposed lack of historical depth; "pastlessness," with the black's supposed lack of a significant past.

13. The essay was entitled "An Absence of Ruins?" the allusion being to (and critical of) Orlando Patterson's 1967 novel, *An Absence of Ruins*.

14. For some considerations of the West Indian writer's relation to history, see variously, Baugh, Walcott, Braithwaite, and McWatt.

15. In point of fact, Herskovits himself was preceded by Morton C. Kahn (1931). Kahn was a student of "public measures as applied to tropical disease" (*Djuka* xvii). While he had visited the "South American tropics" in 1922, 1923, and 1925, visits which "took me to the border of the Bush Negro countries," his first visit to the Djuka was undertaken in 1927, "under the auspices of Dr. Clark Wissler of the Museum of Natural History, [and] with the financial aid of Mr. Myron I. Granger" (xviii). On a second "expedition," in 1928, he was accompanied by Herskovits.

16. See Jackson; I am greatly indebted to this very thoughtful essay. For a recent appreciative reflection on Herskovits, see Fernandez.

17. Indeed this had been the central issue since the end of the Civil War. For a discussion of the debates about the status of Afro-Americans in the post-Reconstruction period, see Meier.

18. In fact, Afro-Americans had earlier developed consciousness of Africa. See, for example Edwin Redkey's study of nineteenth century back-to-Africa movements, *Black Exodus*.

19. Among them were W. E. B. Du Bois, Alain Locke, James Weldon Johnson, and Zora Neale Hurston. Indeed one recent commentator would refer to him as an "honorary New Negro"; he was one of only three white contributors to Alain Locke's *The New Negro* (see Lewis 116).

20. I borrow this phrase from George Stocking (*Ethnographic Sensibility* 209); but see, for example, Herskovits's use of it ("Acculturation" 217; and "Negro" 147).

21. As Herskovits ("Acculturation") points out, the "peculiarly American" term "acculturation" is "not of recent development," but had been used by such prominent American ethnologists as W. J. Powell in the latter part of the nineteenth century. See Stocking's argument ("Franz Boas": 212) that the evolutionist use of it differed greatly from Boas's.

22. Herskovits himself suggests a direct link between his new ideas and the rise of "the New Negro" (see "Negro" 151).

23. He has indeed been critical of just this idea of Herskovits's. See Price ("Saramaka Woodcarving") and Mintz and Price.

24. Or more precisely, the other side of the Boasian conception of culture, which, stressing "pattern," "style," "ethos," had more or less displaced "traits." As Stocking expressed it: "On the one hand, culture was simply an accidental accretion of individual elements. On the other, culture—despite Boas' renunciation of organic growth—was at the same time an integrated spiritual totality that somehow conditioned the form of its elements" ("Franz Boas" 214).

25. See Asad for an instructive deliberation on the concept of "tradition" in relation to Islam.

Works Cited

Appadurai, Arjun. "Theory in Anthropology: Center and Periphery." *Comparative Studies in Society and History* 26.2 (1986): 356–61.

Asad, Talal. *The Idea of an Anthropology of Islam*. Occasional Papers Series. Washington D.C.: Center for Contemporary Arab Studies, 1986.

Baugh, Edward. *Derek Walcott: Memory as Vision: Another Life*. London: Longman, 1978.

———. "The West Indian Writer and his Quarrel with History." *Tapia* 20 Feb. 1977.

Boas, Franz. "The Outlook for the American Negro." *The Shaping of American Anthropology 1883–1911: A Franz Boas Reader*. Ed. George W. Stocking, Jr. New York: Basic, 1974.

———. "The Principles of Ethnological Classification." *The Shaping of American Anthropology 1883–1911: A Franz Boas Reader*. Ed. George W. Stocking, Jr. New York: Basic, 1974.

Borges, Jorge. *Twenty Four Conversations with Borges*. Trans. Nicomedes Suarez Arauz, Willis Barnestone, and Noemi Escandell. New York: Grove, 1984.

Brathwaite, Edward. "Timehri." *Is Massa Day Done?* Ed. Orde Coombs. New York: Anchor, 1974.

Clifford, James. "Introduction: Partial Truths." *Writing Culture: The Poetics and Politics of Ethnography*. Ed. James Clifford and George Marcus. Berkeley: U of California P, 1986.

Du Bois, W. E. B. *Black Folk, Then and Now: An Essay in the History and Sociology of the Negro Race*. New York; Henry Holt, 1939.

———. *The Souls of Black Folk*. 1903. New York: Bantam Books, 1989.

Fernandez, James. W. "Tolerance in a Repugnant World and Other Dilemmas in the Cultural Relativism of Melville J. Herskovits." *Moral Relativism*. Ed. Alan Page Fiske. Spec. issue of *Ethos* 18.2 (1990): 140–64.

Fredrickson, George M. *The Black Image in the White Mind: The Debate of Afro-American Character and Destiny, 1817–1914*. New York: Harper, 1971.

Herskovits, Melville J. "Acculturation and the American Negro." *Southwestern Political and Social Science Quarterly* 8.3 (1927): 211–24.

———. *The Myth of the Negro Past*. New York: Beacon, 1941.

———. "The Negro in the New World: The Statement of a Problem." *American Anthropologist* (ns) 32 (1930): 145–55.

———. "The Negro's Americanism." Locke 353–60.

————. *On Life in a Haitian Valley.* 1937. New York: Anchor, 1971.

Herskovits, Melville, and Frances Herskovits. *Rebel Destiny: Among the Bush Negroes of Dutch Guiana.* 1934. New York: Books for Libraries Press, 1971.

Huggins, Nathan. *Harlem Renaissance.* New York: Oxford UP, 1979.

————, ed. *Voices from the Harlem Renaissance.* New York: Oxford UP, 1976.

Hyatt, Marshall. "Franz Boas and the Struggle for Black Equality: The Dynamics of Ethnicity." *Perspectives in American History* ns 2 (1985): 269–95.

Jackson, Walter. "Melville Herskovits and the Search for Afro-American Culture." *Malinowski, Rivers, Benedict and Others.* Ed. George W. Stocking, Jr. Vol. 4 of *History of Anthropology.* Ed. Stocking. 7 vols. to date. Madison: U of Wisconsin P, 1986.

Kahn, Morton C. *Djuka: The Bush Negroes of Dutch Guiana.* New York: Viking, 1931.

Krupat, Arnold. "Anthropology in the Ironic Mode: The Work of Franz Boas." *Social Text* 19/20 (fall 1988): 105–18.

Lewis, David Levering. *When Harlem was in Vogue.* New York: Oxford UP, 1979.

Locke, Alain, ed. *The New Negro.* New York: Atheneum, 1925.

McGrane, Bernard. *Beyond Anthropology: Society and the Other.* New York: Columbia UP, 1989.

McWatt, Mark. "The Preoccupation with the Past in West Indian Literature." *Caribbean Quarterly* 28.1–2 (1982): 12–19.

Marcus, George E., and Michael M. J. Fischer. *Anthropology as Cultural Critique: An Experimental Moment in the Human Sciences.* Chicago: U of Chicago P, 1986.

Meier, August. *Negro Thought in America, 1880–1915.* Ann Arbor; U of Michigan P, 1963.

Mintz, Sidney W., and Richard Price. *An Anthropological Approach to the Afro-American Past: A Caribbean Perspective.* Philadelphia: Institute for the Study of Human Issues, 1976.

Price, Richard. "An Absence of Ruins?: Seeking Caribbean Historical Consciousness." *Caribbean Review* 14.3 (1985): 24–29, 45.

————. *First-Time: The Historical Vision of an Afro-American People.* Baltimore: Johns Hopkins UP, 1983.

————. *The Guiana Maroons: A Historical and Bibliographical Introduction.* Baltimore: Johns Hopkins UP, 1976.

————. "Saramaka Woodcarving: The Development of an Afroamerican Art." *Man* ns 5.3 (1970): 363–78.

————. *To Slay the Hydra: Dutch Colonial Perspectives on the Saramaka Wars.* Ann Arbor: Karoma Publishers, 1983.

Redfield, Robert, Ralph Linton, and Melville J. Herskovits. "Memorandum for the Study of Acculturation." *American Anthropologist* ns 38 (1936): 149–52.

Redkey, Edwin S. *Black Exodus: Black Nationalist and Back-to-Africa Movements, 1890–1910.* New Haven: Yale UP, 1969.

Rosaldo, Renato. "Doing Oral History." *Social Analysis* 4 (1980): 89–99.

———. *Ilongot Headhunting, 1883–1974*. Stanford: Stanford UP, 1980.

Schomburg, Arthur. "The Negro Digs up his Past." Locke 231–37.

Stocking, George W., Jr. "Anthropology as *Kulturkampf*: Science and Politics in the Career of Franz Boas." *The Uses of Anthropology*. Ed. Walter Goldschmidt Washington DC: American Anthropological Association, 1979.

———. "The Ethnographic Sensibility of the 1920s and the Dualism of the Anthropological Tradition." *Romantic Motives: Essays on Anthropological Sensibility*. Ed. George W. Stocking Jr. Vol. 6 of *History of Anthropology*. Ed. Stocking. 7 vols. to date. Madison: U of Wisconsin P, 1989.

———. "Franz Boas and the Culture Concept in Historical Perspective." *Race, Culture, and Evolution: Essays in the History of Anthropology*. Chicago: U of Chicago P, 1968.

Szwed, John F. "An American Anthropological Dilemma: The Politics of Afro-American Culture." *Reinventing Anthropology*. Ed. Dell Hymes. New York: Vintage, 1974.

Walcott, Derek. "The Muse of History." *Is Massa Day Done?* Ed. Orde Coombs. New York: Anchor, 1974.

White, Hayden. "Interpretation in History." *Tropics of Discourse: Essays in Cultural Criticism*. Baltimore: Johns Hopkins UP, 1978.

Willis, William. "Anthropology and Negroes on the Southern Colonial Frontier." *The Black Experience in America: Selected Essays*. Ed. James C. Curtis and Lewis L. Gould Austin: U of Texas P, 1970.

Diaspora 1:3 1991

The Poetics and Practice of Iranian Nostalgia in Exile

Hamid Naficy
University of California, Los Angeles

1. Nostalgia as Cultural Practice

In this article, I will focus on the poetics and practice of nostalgia in exilic popular culture, drawing primarily on examples from some 10 years of Iranian television programs and music videos produced in Los Angeles. Nostalgia, a feature of exile, has in recent years become a "cultural practice" and a "mode of representation" (K. Stewart 227, 238) as postmodernity, neocolonialism, communism, totalitarianism, imperialism, and transnational capital have displaced peoples and cultures the world over. Fredric Jameson tells us that this fragmentation and deterritorialization forces us to experience time differently; that is, we experience the present as a loss or, as Baudrillard would have it, as a phenomenon that has no origin or reality, a "hyperreality" (2). For the exiles who have emigrated from Third World countries, life in the United States, especially in the quintessentially postmodern city of Los Angeles, is doubly unreal, and it is because of this double loss—of origin and of reality—that nostalgia becomes a major cultural and representational practice among the exiles. In addition, nostalgia for one's homeland has a fundamentally interpsychic source expressed in the trope of an eternal desire for return—a return that is structurally unrealizable. Freud speaks of homesickness as a longing for a return to the womb of the motherland, and Jane Gallop asserts:

> If we understand the nostalgia resulting from the discovery of the mother's castration in this way, then the discovery that the mother does not have the phallus means that the subject can never return to the womb. Somehow the fact that the mother is not phallic means that the mother as mother is lost forever, that the mother as womb, homeland, source, and grounding for the subject is irretrievably past. The subject is hence in a foreign land, alienated. (148)

Although the lost mother is structurally irretrievable, the lost homeland is potentially recoverable and it is this potentiality—however imaginary—that drives the exiles' multifaceted desire to return.

2. Return to the Origin

For some, separation from and loss of the homeland is a deliberate choice that indicates a desire to escape from the ravages of both a patriarchal family and a social order prevalent in the home country. For many, however, grief over forced separation and loss is unresolvable and thus leads to depression and dysphoria (Good, Good, and Moradi 391). As I have argued elsewhere ("Televisual"), some people disavow loss and separation either through creating and controlling fetishes or creating and submitting to fetishes. For others, the disavowal of loss and separation is supplanted by an impulse to return, to reunite with the object of the fetish, the (m)otherland; to regress into the prelapsarian narcissism of childhood; to reestablish the communal self. This is a characteristic that sets exiles apart from all other displaced people, such as expatriates and immigrants. Indeed, "exile is a dream of glorious return" (Rushdie 205), a dream that as Freud and Lacan predicted remains alluring only as long as it remains unrealized.

We must consider the paradigm of exile as it operates within the exiles' native culture, because it is through that paradigm that they think and experience their lives in exile. For Iranians, it is poetry, especially sufi (mystic) poetry, that provides the paradigmatic worldview and language of exile, embodying a variety of journeys, returns, and unifications. Such an assertion may seem implausible to readers unfamiliar with Iranian culture; certainly, a similar claim about any contemporary western culture would not be upheld. However, as historians, anthropologists, literary critics, and any number of Iranians can attest, theirs is a culture suffused by poetry and shaped by the citation of canonical, classical (and at times contemporary) poets in daily life; rich and poor can and do cite Ferdowsi, Sa'adi, Hafez, Rumi, and Khayyam. The paradigm of exile is indissolubly linked with the *Hejri* calendar, the Iranian version of the Muslim *Hijrah* (*hegira*), dating from the prophet Mohammad's emigration to Medina, which was followed some years later by a triumphant return to Mecca. The exiled poet Nader Naderpour has classified the notion of *hegira* (emigration) as a multilayered metaphor for 1) exile (hegira from one's country), 2) life itself (hegira from Eden), 3) passage to adulthood (hegira from childhood), 4) acquisition of knowledge and insight (hegira from innocence), and 5) the daily passage of the sun (hegira from dawn to dusk). Clearly, exile is a palimpsest inscribed with many layers of meanings and is deeply rooted in the culture and psyche of Iranians. While Nader-pour's formulation is in line with the Iranian mystical tradition (of sufism), it nevertheless misses the importance of that central notion which turns migration into exile animated by the desire for return and reunion—a concept deeply encoded in Iranian mysticism and the psychic structure discussed as *safa-ye baten* (inner purity).

This mystic paradigm of exile fits the Lacanian formulation of the permanent disruption of prelapsarian unified wholeness, or the Imaginary, by the entry of the child into the Symbolic order (culture and language); this disruption inclines humans forever after to seek to recover wholeness, to identify and to become one with the Imaginary. Classic figures of Iranian mystical poetry, such as Farid al-Din Attar and Jalal al-Din Rumi, have elaborated these notions of exile in their masterpieces.[1] Nowhere is the pain of separation and the longing for return and reunification expressed more passionately than in Rumi's famous "The Song of the Reed," a portion of which, translated by William Jones, reads:

> Hear, how yon reed in sadly pleasing tales
> Departed bliss and present woe bewails!
> "With me, from native banks untimely torn,
> Love-warbling youths and soft-ey'ed virgins mourn.
> O! let the heart, by fatal absence rent,
> Feel what I sing, and bleed when I lament;
> Who roams in exile from his parent bow'r,
> Pants to return, and chides each ling'ring hour.
> My notes, in circles of the grave and gay,
> Have hail'd the rising, cheer'd the closing day:
> Each in my fond affections claim'd a part,
> But none discern'd the secret of my heart.
> What though my strains and sorrows flow combine'd!
> Yet ears are slow, and carnal eyes are blind.
> Free through each mortal form the spirits roll,
> But sight avails not. Can we see the soul?"
> Such notes breath'd gently from yon vocal frame:
> Breath'd said I? no; 'twas all enliv'ning flame.
> 'Tis love, that fills the reed with warmth divine;
> 'Tis love, that sparkles in the racy wine.
> Me, plaintive wand'rer from my peerless maid,
> The reed has fir'd, and all my soul betray'd.
> He gives the bane, and he with balsam cures;
> Afflicts, yet soothes; impassions, yet allures.
> Delightful pangs his amo'rous tales prolong;
> And Laili's frantick lover lives in song.
>
> (Arberry 118–19)

This complicated, mystical, painful yet alluring paradigm of exile still informs and infuses the discourse of Iranians in the United States who, like the lamenting reed in Rumi's poem, long for a return to their homeland—a longing intensified by the inability of many to return.[2] The novelist Mahshid Amirshahi, who lives in France, uses a botanical metaphor to speak of the inevitability and the pain of this longing:

> More than belonging to the future, I am grafted to the earth. I am searching for a lost earth in which I am rooted, a sun in whose rays I have gained strength, and a water by whose grace I have matured. No matter how wasted this earth, how burning this sun, and how meager this water, I love them. . . . I will return to this land, this earth, this homeland. (45)

The literary critic Farzaneh Milani, in a poem called "Zadqah" (Birthplace), invokes a biological metaphor, in which she draws a parallel between the inevitability of the longing of the exiles for a return to their homeland and the biological urge of salmon to return to their spawning grounds. For her, that biological urge is a voice that calls and recalls, beckoning the exiles onward toward joyous reunion (Milani 26). Both Amirshahi and Milani, however, like Naderpour, overlook an important feature of the exile paradigm, namely the fact that the unconsummated longing which is the motive force of this art would cease to exist if return and reunion were successfully accomplished.[3] The impossibility of return and reunion are fundamental elements of human signification; as Susan Stewart has noted,

> The inability of the sign to "capture" its signified, of narrative to be one with its object, and of genres of mechanical reproduction to approximate the time of face-to-face communication leads to a generalized desire for origin, for nature, for unmediated experience that is at work in nostalgic longing. (23–24)

The same inability to "capture" the homeland is operative in exilic discourse; without distance, without separation, the nostalgic longing so prominent in exile would not be: "It is in this gap between resemblance and identity that nostalgic desire arises. *The nostalgia is enamored of distance, not of the referent itself* (S. Stewart 145, emphasis added).[4] The "glorious return," the operative engine of actively maintained exile, must remain unrealized; in the words of Rumi, the exile must roam and pant to return but never actually achieve it.

The nostalgia remains, then, and this nostalgia, this desire to desire, is staged narratologically in music videos frequently aired by exile television.[5] In one video, for example, aired on the *Midnight Show* (KSCI-TV, Los Angeles, 27 Mar. 1988), the singer Sattar sings about departing from home but leaving his heart with his family, which has remained behind. As he sings in exile about loss and separation, a family group photo, apparently taken in Iran in his absence, appears behind him. At this point, the image of Sattar singing, which had dominated the foreground, gradually grows smaller until it fits in a spot inside the group photo in the background. The foreground fuses with the background. The gap between resemblance and identity is filled in. The singer has found his rightful place in the family photo and is thereby symbolically reunited with his kin. If reunion is not possible physically, it at least can be staged metaphorically. Thus, the ever-threatening loss is averted and the lack is filled in metaphorically, the pain assuaged symbolically.

However, this nostalgic past is itself ideological in that, as Said writes in *Orientalism* (55), it has become an "imaginary geography," a construction created by exilic narratives. But this construction is not hermetic, since the "real" past threatens to reproduce itself as a lack or loss: it is against the threat of such a loss that the nostalgic past must be turned into a series of nostalgic objects, into fetish-souvenirs that can be displayed and consumed repeatedly. Photo albums, letters, diaries, telephones, birds in flight, candles, rising smoke from cigarettes or from fog machines, the beach and the waves of the ocean—these are some of the nostalgic fetishes circulated in music videos. Images of people looking through photo albums, reading and writing letters in the light of a candle, of a burning cigarette smoking in an unattended ash tray, of loved ones conversing on the phone—these are the recurring micronarratives of nostalgic return.

Such fetish-souvenirs, and the narratives in which they are embedded, have a dual role: they serve to authenticate a past and simultaneously to discredit the present. Their authenticating function can be understood better if a parallel is drawn with religious and secular rituals, during which, as Victor Turner has observed,

> often, but not always, myths are recited explaining the origin, attributes, and behavior of these strange and sacred habitants of liminality. Again, sacred objects may be shown to the novices. These may be quite simple in form like the bone, top, ball, tambourine, apples, mirror, fan, and woolly fleece displayed in the lesser Eleusinian mysteries of Athens. Such *sacra*, individually or in various combinations, may be the foci of hermeneutics or religious interpretations, sometimes in the form of myths, sometimes of gnomic utterances hardly less enigmatic than the visible symbols they purport to explain. (*Dramas* 239)

These souvenirs, fetishes, icons, symbols, and narratives along with the Persian art and craft objects imported from home, which dominate the interior spaces of home in exile, operate as cultural mnemonics, through the circulation of which the "habitants of liminality," namely, the exiles, attempt to transmit to "novices," that is, to their children, who are fast becoming American, the parents' native cosmologies and values, which they feel are under threat. What is more, to paraphrase Kathleen Stewart, the Persian art and crafts objects that decorate the exiles' homes do not so much *reproduce* Iran as *produce* a world made of signs: "The point is not just to 'decorate' in itself but to signify the production, or at least the possibility, of meaning" (233). The meaning that is produced involves establishing both cultural and ethnic differentiation (from the host society) and cultural and ethnic continuity (with an idealized past and the homeland); in short, what is at stake here is the construction of what Bourdieu has called the codes of "distinction and taste" (*Distinction*). These objets d'art and handicrafts, which decorate the homes, and the variety of food items available in the grocery stores and restaurants help to produce and validate in exile, to borrow from Herbert Gans, a distinctively Persian "taste culture."

However, by focusing almost solely on vision (and more recently on sound), film and television studies have failed to develop theories that can account for the relationship between film and television and the other senses of the human sensorium. The exiles construct their difference through not just what they see and hear but through their senses of smell, taste, and touch. Indeed, these aspects of the sensorium often provide, even more than sight and hearing, poignant markers and reminders of difference and of separation from homeland and therefore must be considered seriously.

Exile is a contentious state, and the feelings of community and unification produced by these fetishes and souvenirs are disrupted by the dilemmas of hesitation, ambivalence, and indeterminacy, which mark all exiles. Sattar's music video, *Safarnameh* (travelog), aired on *Parsian* TV (KSCI-TV, 22 Sept. 1984), is an apt example. He is seated next to a piano in a comfortable living room in the United States, paging through a book (an album of photographs or a diary). As he sings and thumbs through the book, we see images of Iran: pigeon towers in verdant fields, tea groves, diggers of *qanats* (subterranean water channels), tribal women, a shepherd boy and his flock of sheep. The visuals invoke fetishized souvenirs of a past—indeed, of a primarily rural Iran that is not in the background of the mostly urban emigrants from Iran—and the lyrics speak of the hardship of the emigration journey and of its metaphoric documentation in the diary: "My pen is my feet and my diary book is the long stretch of the road I have traveled." The contradiction between the visuals, which emphasize unity with the homeland, and the lyrics, which highlight separation and exile, crystalizes in the last few lines, in which he speaks of a tortured ambivalence:

> I am caught in the dead end of doubt and irresolution:
> Which of these two paths is mine?
> Help me, Oh love, so I may not perish in exile.

3. Return to Nature

When return is not possible in actuality, and when its metaphorical and narratological staging is found to be insufficient, other substitutes may be sought. Liminality itself, as Turner tells us, is a timeless condition, which places "enhanced stress on nature at the expense of culture" (*Dramas:* 252). It does so by invoking the biological and the symbolic processes of the natural order. In the absence of the native habitus—that is, the former social, political, familial, linguistic structures, and authorities of home—the exile culture now is forced to seek the structures and the kind of authority that only nature is thought to be capable of providing: timelessness, boundlessness, predictability, reliability, stability, and universality. That is why Iranian music videos are filled with images of the land, mountains, fields, sky, setting sun, sea, and monuments so ancient that they have acquired the status of a natural phenomenon (e.g., Persepolis). Most Iranian music videos contain visuals of nature and lyrics about love which, because of their ambiguity, can be interpreted as depicting love of any kind, that is, a universal love resulting in longing for origin, home, family, country, and, since the pronouns of the Persian language are not gender specific, either homosexual or heterosexual love.

Exile television programs, especially music videos, are heavily coded with nature, particularly the sea. An example is a music video called *Parandush* (name of a bird or a girl), aired on *Cheshmak* TV (KSCI-TV, 31 Jan. 1989) and sung by a female singer, Zoya. We see the singer perched on the rocks overlooking the ocean, singing about the lost bird of the title, complaining that "the pain of separation from you has turned my heart into a sea." The lyrics are clearly about love—a love that variously can be taken to be for a bird, Zoya's family, her lover, her country.[6] Visually, Zoya is made one with the sea: her image is superimposed over the waves, giving it the appearance of either hovering faintly above the waves or washing gently to the shore with them. Her dissolution into the sea is enhanced by the manner in which the soundtrack is created: her voice, the solo piano accompanying her, and the sound of waves washing or crashing against the shore are so delicately intermingled as to create a union. Another music video, *Ashena* (familiar), aired on *Neqah* TV (KSCI-TV) and sung by a male singer, Davoud, shows the singer achieving a kind of visual and epistemological symbiosis with the sea. He seems to have become the ocean itself, his image alternately floating on the surface of the water or submerged just below the surface. Throughout, his image and that of the waves interact and interweave, while the love song intones: "Oh, always familiar, stay with me, tell me your thoughts, make me yours." Again, ambiguities make possible a number of readings, but clearly the preferred reading coded in the video is the union, through dissolution, with mother nature.[7]

The land, literally the earth of Iran, also figures importantly in music videos. For example, Homa Mirafshar has produced a book of poetry accompanied by a videocassette, entitled *Alaleh* (Buttercup), which contains a number of videopoems about exile and separation and is accompanied by music. One of these videopoems, aired on *Jam-e Jam* TV (KSCI-TV, 27 Nov. 1988), shows a montage of clips from Albert Lamorisse's film on Iran, *The Lovers' Wind* (1969). The visuals show a variety of Iranian landscapes and geological formations while the lyrics, recited by the poet, speak of undying love for the country and for the land:

> You are the best reason for my continued existence
> You are love's refuge, a warm roof over a home
> You are a love ballad, an eternal song
> Live long O land of Iran.

Here it is necessary to recall and analyze briefly Lamorisse's film, which constructs Iran as *nature itself*: timeless, boundless, permanent, and filled with wondrous natural beauty. Most of the footage, filmed from a hovering helicopter, represents the point of view of the various winds (e.g., warm, crimson, evil, and lovers' winds) which "inhabit" the land and which anthropomorphically "narrate" the film.

> The camera, defying gravity with smoothness and agility, provides a bird's-eye-view, caressing minarets and domes, peeking over and beyond mountain tops, gliding over remote villages to reveal the life enclosed within high, mud-brick walls, leaping along with the local wildlife, following the rhythmic, sinuous flow of the oil pipelines and train tracks, and hovering over the mirror-like mosaic of the rice terraces that reflect the clouds and sky. (Naficy, *Iran Media* xvii)

As we see these images, we hear the mellifluous voice of a narrator who, speaking on behalf of each wind, narrates portions of the film in the first person. The images of natural landscapes, "naturized" human-made monuments, and the narrative points of view of the winds all link Iran directly with natural elements and with nature itself, thus providing a testimonial to the obduracy, resilience, and permanence of Iran and of the Iranian people. In times of exilic stress and self-doubt, such images are most reassuring, as the constant and continued plundering and plagiarization of clips from *The Lovers' Wind* by Iranian filmmakers serve to underscore. Program logos, music videos, videopoems, and documentaries on exiles all repeatedly employ clips from this film.

The union with "mother nature" encoded in these videos is a symbolic substitute for reunion with the "natural mother" and with the "motherland," which is currently impossible for many of the exiles (and for all of the singers of pop music because of the vehement opposition of the Iranian government to this genre of music on account of its putative amoral and corrupting influences). Videos vicariously and nostalgically transfer the primarily bourgeois exiles to their childhood, to their past, and to the "good old times" by the Caspian Sea. These references to nature might be read also as attempts at activating senses other than vision and hearing in order to reproduce that intangible "feel" of the homeland.

As part of the iconographic encyclopedia of nature, both the *Ashena* and the *Parandush* videos show birds in flight alternately as symbols of the journey, of escape, of freedom, of messages borne over long distances. The image of a white dove as a signifier for peace is well known, an image used particularly effectively as an opening logo by a program called *Sima-ye Azadi* (Face of freedom). We see a white dove frozen in flight against a solid blue sky, and we hear the crescendo sequence of Strauss's *Also Sprach Zarathustra,* as in the soundtrack of Stanley Kubrick's *2001: A Space Odyssey,* at which time the title of the show is keyed in. The semiotic and ideological skirmish at work becomes clear upon scrutinizing the political subtexts.

The program is produced by the Mojahedin, an Iranian guerrilla group headquartered in Iraq. The group is opposed both to the return of monarchy to Iran and to the present Islamic government; it claims itself to be the sole legitimate alternative. As a result, the group can use neither the pre-Islamic, Achaemeneid iconography monopolized by the royalists nor the Islamic one exclusively employed by the current regime in Iran. But, since warfare is impossible without ideological and semiotic mobilization, the organization has opted for the white dove of freedom to differentiate itself and its politics from both the royalists and the Islamic clerics now in power. Significantly, in all cases, the supporters of the monarchy, the present Islamic government, and the Mojahedin are appealing to the symbolism and the iconography that predate the existence of the factions themselves and, in some ways, link them to the natural or cosmological order.

In the same way that a bird in flight is seen as a symbol of freedom, a caged bird signifies imprisonment—an image with a long-standing tradition in Iranian mysticism, literature, and cinema.[8] Many music videos and audiocassettes produced in exile refer to exile as imprisonment. One episode of the avant-garde television program Khorus-e Bimahal (KSCI-TV, 14 Oct. 1989) constantly repeats a close-up image of a caged bird both in the background, behind the host, and in the foreground. As befits the style of the show, there is no commentary, but periodically a hand reaches into the frame and pats the top of the cage, thus drawing attention to it. At times, it seems as though the host himself is inside the cage. At times, too, the cage is empty, and the perch swings back and forth, signifying flight and escape. The feelings of freedom, refuge, and imprisonment that exile implies all are encoded in this show.

"Naturization" can be an effective political ploy in the semiotic and ideological power struggle in exile, a process that, for example, has turned the Ayatollah Ruhollah Khomeini himself into a wild or dangerous mythical beast. He is called, among other things, old hyena (*kaftar-e pir*), vampire bat (*khoffash-e khun asham*), ominous owl (*joghd-e shum*), anti-Christ (*dajjal*), fire-breathing dragon (*ezhdaha*), Chinese female demon (*efriteh-ye Machin*), and Zahhak (a king in Persian mythology who grew two snakes on his shoulders, which had to be fed with the brains of young people). The popular press in exile has dubbed Khomeini's regime "octopus" (*okhtapus*) and "the plague" (*ta'un*). Even his own demonic characterization of the United States as "the great satan" (*shaitan-e bozorg*) has been turned against him in the exile media.[9] Anthropology has shown us that liminal states, whether the Iranian revolutionary culture itself, which produced the Great Satan label originally, or the exilic polity that recycles it, require the invocation of existing beast images or the creation of new theranthropic and ornithanthropic monsters, whose real or imagined threat can serve to mobilize the entire society. Such monsterization of the United States by Khomeini, and of Khomeini and the ruling clerics in Iran by the exiles, is productive in the sense that it turns the sacred into the profane and at the same time theoretically serves to turn the chaos of revolution in the former case and the condition of exile in the latter case into a safe, symbolic *communitas*.

4. Symbolic Construction of Ethnicity and Nationality

Communitas implies that members of the exile community share something with one another that distinguishes them from others and that helps them to maintain ethnic solidarity and ideological integrity. The exiles accomplish this by establishing and maintaining similarities through elaboration of differences based on ethnicity and locality—a practice that flies in the face of attempts made by structuralists to negate the concept of community in favor of universal structures. We are in a historical period characterized by the collapse of traditional universalist ideologies such as colonialism, neocolonialism, and communism, and we are witnessing the world over, in preindustrial and postindustrial nations alike, people who continue to assert aggressively their locality and ethnicity through the marking of their boundaries.[10] Such boundaries are 1) largely symbolically constructed, 2) sometimes imperceptible to outsiders, 3) redefinable by the members of the community itself, and 4) maintained through manipulation of symbols of that community. In short, "the reality and the efficacy of the community's boundary— and, therefore, of the community itself—depends upon its symbolic construction and embellishment" (Cohen 15).

Rituals provide the terrain in which the consciousness of communal boundaries is heightened, thereby confirming and strengthening individual location and positionality as well as social identity. As such, rituals are important means of experiencing the self as a communal self, and that is why rituals of celebration (weddings, bar mitzvahs, discos, political demonstrations, anniversaries, calendrical celebrations) occupy such a prominent place in the cultural repertoire of the exiles, through which they affirm and reinforce their communal boundaries. Exile television can itself be considered a "ritual" that functions in parallel with other boundary-maintaining practices. The concept of television as a ritual is complex; suffice it to say that television is a ritual chiefly because, similar to other forms of rituals, it brings order and a sense of control to the life of the viewer by producing, replicating, and regulating a variety of systematic patterns which set up expectations that are continually fulfilled: narratological and generic patterns (program format, formulaic story lines, stock characters, regular program hosts and newscasters, setting), patterns of consumption (the scheduled airing and repeated airing of programs, interruption of the narrative for commercials), and patterns of signification (iconography, meaning production) (Turner *Symbols*; Carpenter; Myerhoff).

Rituals gain additional prominence when the actual social boundaries of the community are being undermined, blurred, or weakened. The liminality of exile is one such situation in which the integrity of all boundaries (of the self, of the ethnic group, or of the nation) is problematized, and it is to deal with such a threat that exile television becomes a boundary-maintaining symbolic ritual as it constructs through fetishization an electronic *communitas* that bestows a sense of stability and commonality to the exiles. Moreover, such a fetishized *communitas* is augmented by "webs of significance" (Geertz 5), which the exiles spin around themselves through the popular culture they produce and consume—a culture that is not so much imposed upon the exiles by the host society as it is created, renegotiated, and recreated continually, through social interaction among the exiles themselves. As in fetishization, part of the function of popular culture is to produce a repository of symbols, a web of signification, through which exiles can differentiate themselves from the host society. That is why exile is such an intensely symbolic and semiotic space:

> The community itself and everything within it, conceptual as well as material, has a symbolic dimension; and, further . . . this dimension does not exist as some kind of consensus of sentiment. Rather, it exists as something for people "to think with." The symbols of a community are mental constructs: they provide people with the means to make meaning. In so doing, they also provide them with the means to express the particular meanings which the community has for them. (Cohen 19)

Nostalgia propagated by means of exile-produced television programs, artifacts, souvenirs, and narratives of return and reunion with the motherland and with nature are ways in which immigrant communities in exile mark their ethnic boundaries.

Nationalism, too, becomes a forceful method of marking one's exilic boundaries and of promoting solidarity. Nationalism is associated intrinsically with exile, because "all nationalisms in their early stages posit as their goal the overcoming of some estrangement—from soil, from roots, from unity, from destiny" (Said, "Life in Exile" 50). Moreover, exile encourages nationalism because it affirms belonging not just to a place but also to what Bourdieu has called "habitus," a community of language, customs, dispositions, and "structured structures predisposed to function as structuring structures" (*Outline* 72). There is, however, a drawback to these formulations. Intense focalization on and overinvestment in the fetish demands that the fetish and its synecdoche remain pure, unsullied, unambiguous, irreproachable, and authentic. This, in turn, can lead to a shortsighted form of nationalism (chauvinism) and to racially prejudiced stances, evident in the discourse of Iranian exile media, which insist on distinct authenticity, historical antiquity, and racial difference (especially vis-à-vis Arabs). In this manner, the media, especially television, produce in exile a cultural artifact, an imaginary nation, or as formulated by Benedict Anderson, an "imagined community" that is conceived as inherently limited and secularly sovereign (15–16).[11] This is so because in the discourse of Iranian exile television, which is primarily royalist, nothing is more sacred than "Iran" itself, a homeland that has actually undergone rapid fundamental change under the Islamic Republic, but whose televisual simulacrum in exile (imagined as nature) remained generally stable (limited), at least during the war with Iraq. In addition, this "authentic" homeland (community), memorialized through fetishization and nostalgic longing, is usually projected as a secular, non-Islamic (sovereign) community.[12]

Anderson identifies the "national novel" and the newspaper with its focus on calendrical events as chief shapers of national consciousness. For the Iranian exiles, however, living in Los Angeles and in some other diasporan communities large enough to have their own television programs, and dwelling in a highly mediated postindustrial society like the United States, it is the popular culture they produce and consume, especially television, that circulates nationalist consciousness. Because exile television's contribution to the formation of this consciousness occurs at a distance, it works not only synchronically (to produce horizontal comradeship among the exiles and those at home) but also diachronically (bridging the temporal gap between those living in exile and at home). The physical distance between Iran and the United States creates not only a difference of time zones (some 12 hours between Iran and the West Coast of the United States) but also a feeling that Islamicized Iran is living in (or even reliving) a different historical epoch. Exile television bridges these dual gaps: the exiles—distanced spatially—are made synchronous temporally.

But what are they made synchronous with? The answer is, with an "invented tradition," in the sense employed by the historian Eric Hobsbawm:

> "Invented tradition" is taken to mean a set of practices, normally governed by overtly or tacitly accepted rules and of a ritual or symbolic nature, which seek to inculcate certain values and norms of behavior by repetition [and] automatically [imply] continuity with the past. In fact, where possible, they normally attempt to establish continuity with a suitable historic past. (Hobsbawm 1)

The past that exile television has found suitable as its reference point is chiefly the pre-Islamic past, in whose fetishes are encoded the values of Iranian antiquity, historicity, national chauvinism, patriotism, and superiority, and which are repeatedly circulated within exile television's political economy.[13] Hobsbawm makes the point that when social patterns are weakened or destroyed, as in time of exile, the impulse to invent traditions increases. He cites three types of traditions invented since the industrial revolution: 1) those establishing or symbolizing social cohesion, 2) those establishing or legitimizing institutions, status, and authority, and 3) those establishing socialization and reinforcing inculcation of beliefs, values, and behavior (Hobsbawm 9). Over the years, the communitarian type (the first type above) of invented tradition has tended to dominate, and it seems to dominate in exile as well. Its chief purposes seem to be to legitimize the past, to cement group solidarity in the present, and to guide political action in the future. That is why television and music videos place so much emphasis on the display of the national flag, the national anthem, and national emblems such as the map of Iran.

Citing Ernest Renan's formulation, Gellner asserts that "a shared amnesia, a collective forgetfulness, is . . . essential for the emergence of what we now consider to be a nation" (6). The aesthetics and politics of national chauvinism and fetishization discussed so far are based on partial repression of the reality of Iran and of the past; in that sense, they could be construed to be forms of amnesia engendered by exile. It is through this collective repressing/forgetting or deliberate misreading of the past that the exiles can symbolically create a sense of communal cohesion and ethnic solidarity.

This collective identity, however, is not a prior condition; rather, it is a "continually constituted and reconstructed category" (Schlesinger 260). Exile as a process of becoming necessarily entails not a fixed position or location but positionality and locations. What this means is that the form of nationalism and national consciousness now evident surely will undergo modification in time. As Hall astutely points out:

> [C]ultural identity is not a fixed essence at all, lying unchanged outside history and culture. It is not some universal and transcendental spirit inside us on which history has made no fundamental mark. It is not once-and-for-all. It is not a fixed origin to which we can make some final and absolute return. Of course, it is not a mere phantom, either. It is *something*—not a mere trick of the imagination. It has histories—and histories have their real, material and symbolic effects. The past continues to speak to us. But this is no longer a simple, factual "past," since our relation to it is, like the child's relation to the mother, always-already "after the break". It is always constructed through memory, fantasy, narrative and myth. Cultural identities are the points of identification, the unstable points of identification or suture, which are made within the discourses of history and culture. (71–72)

My discussion of ethnic solidarity and nationalism cannot be complete without noting the contradictions that will inevitably exist between the notion of the past and of history that the exiles have produced for themselves, and those imagined by the people living in the home country. Both are imaginary and invented; coming from different positionalities and locations (in time and space), they will continue to diverge. The exilic commonality with home, then, is illusory. It must also be noted that the style of imagining is not homogeneous, that there are different versions of history: official versions and those held in popular memory. At home the official history is promulgated by mainline media; in Iranian exile, a kind of exilic official history is propagated by largely royalist producers and consumers. This nostalgic longing and its cultural artifacts and processes in exile entail regressive practices. It is true that nostalgia can also be motivated by a realistic perception of decline of the present time, of shock in the future to come, of deterritorialization and displacement, or by crises of identity; it is also true that nostalgia serves to soften the blows from these various traumas. Nonetheless, in the final analysis it is regressive, because it seeks not so much to preserve the past as to restore it through fetishization of an idealized construction. Politically, nostalgic longing can produce not unity but discord, not peace but war. Even worse, under certain conditions, "a politics of nostalgia leads to a politics of genocide" (Dasenbrock 317).[14]

Like all official histories/stories, the exilic ones are neither homogeneous nor fixed for long, since exile itself is processual in that it flows in history and changes with time. Other histories/stories are generated and circulated in other exile media with which television develops sympathetic and dissonant resonances. This conception of exile community as a culture that produces and consumes a variety of meanings and cultures contrasts sharply with functionalist and "integrative" traditions, such as the one expounded by Durkheim, whose central conception of society was one that procured solidarity by subsuming differences and by forming indissoluble bonds among members. Indeed, both the intracommunal (within the exile community) and intercommunal bonds (with the host society) are in considerable dialectical tension. Nostalgia in exile engenders ethnic solidarity and ideological stability, but, at the same time, it inscribes ambiguities, contradictions, and instabilities.

Notes

1. Shihabuddin Yahya Suhrawardi, the founder of the theosophical-philosophical illuminationist school in the twelfth century, in his treatise "A Tale of Occidental Exile" provides a discourse on these themes.

2. The vein of the discourse of mysticism as spelled out by Rumi has been productively explored by artists in exile. For example, an entire issue (no. 3, 1989) of *Seda-ye Shahr,* the audio magazine, was devoted to Rumi's poetry; the musical compositions of avant-garde performance artist Susan Daihim, who lives in New York, are much influenced by him, as are the sculptural works of Shirazeh Hushiari, who works in London (for an interview with Hushiari, see Morgan). The

short, poetic film *Nafir* (Plaintive song, 1982), made by Jahanshah Ardalan in San Francisco, takes its title and its poetic sensibilities from Rumi's "Song of the Reed," quoted here. Nahid Rachlin's exile novel, *Foreigner,* defying Freud, Lacan, and Rumi, stages not only the return of an Iranian émigré woman to her motherland but also her reunion with her long-lost biological mother.

3. Rachlin's novel *Foreigner* suffers precisely from her unproblematical staging of such a complete and total reunion.

4. This is also true of maroon societies founded by black African slaves in Brazil, as Bastide notes: "Maroonage involved more a nostalgia for Africa than an exact reconstitution of it . . . for new geographical, demographic, and political conditions obtained and these had to be dealt with" (199).

5. I refer to "exile TV" and thereby elide discussion of an Iranian diaspora or immigrant or transnational community, though all of these are terms that can be validly applied to portions of the Los Angeles community. Many Iranians committed to staying in the West and to a certain degree of assimilation, though very few Iranians desire full assimilation. The concept of return, which I discuss here in terms of exile, is exactly central to diasporan consciousness, and the Iranian community of Los Angeles is a transnational and liminal community, actively in touch, across the borders of nation-states, with the homeland and with Iranians living elsewhere, for example, in London, Stockholm, and Paris.

6. The Persian expression *darya del* (sea hearted) refers to an individual who is magnanimous (openhanded) or courageous (lionhearted). This music video seems not to refer to this expression, but to the homology between a heart beating for a loved one and a tumultuous sea separating the exiles from their homelands. The exile heart is a pulsating sea, pounding on both shores.

7. This type of union with the sea as enacted in music videos is highly suggestive of the earliest infant-mother relationship once called, appropriately, the "oceanic feeling." Nowadays, this union is called symbiosis. On oceanic feeling, see Masson.

8. A good cinematic example is the film *Dash Akol* (1969) directed by Mas'ud Kimia'i and based on a short story by Sadeq Hedayat. In the film, a caged lovebird symbolizes many things, among them, the love the *luti* ("tough guy") Dash Akol feels for his ward, Marjan, his sense of being imprisoned by that love, and his feeling of having become confined as a result of accepting the obligation of guardianship. The caged bird may also symbolize Marjan, who is confined by both patriarchy and religious tradition. For more details, see Naficy, "Iranian Writers."

9. For an analysis of the evolution and significance of the concept of the Great Satan, see Beeman.

10. This has left two remaining universalist projects confronting each other: western liberal democracy and resurgent Islam.

11. Imagined communities can be found in many parts of the world. For example, two films, *Ori* (1989) and *Quilombo* (1984), document and recreate respectively the rise and fall and the continued significance for blacks living in Brazil of pioneer exile communities called Quilombo de Palmares. Although annihilated by the whites, these communities still are held as archetypes of ideal free slave communities.

12. For my theoretical account and iconographic analysis of the role of fetishization in exilic television, see Naficy, "Televisual Fetishization."

13. On the development of nationalism in Iran up to the revolution of 1978–79, see Cottam.

14. Witness the Nazis' savagery in the name of a nostalgic return to an idealized racial construction. Witness also the more recent "high crimes and misdemeanors," to deploy the phrase used in presidential impeachment proceedings, which were committed by the U.S. government in the recent Persian Gulf war, partly justified by a nostalgic return to earlier primal scenes two centuries apart: the American war of independence against the British and the American war against Vietnam. The nostalgia for the success in the former and fear of the repetition of defeat

in the latter energized the drive to pulverize the Iraqi economic and industrial infrastructure, allowing the president and the mainline media to declare the "Vietnam syndrome" dead. Recall President Bush's oft-repeated remark: This fight is for the independence of Kuwait, it is not another Vietnam war. True enough, but was the war not justified as an attempt partially to restore the nostalgic image of an undefeated United States?

Works Cited

Amirshahi, Mahshid. "Dar Safar." *Asheghaneh* 44 (December 1988): 44–45.

Anderson, Benedict. *Imagined Communities: Reflections on the Origin and Spread of Nationalism*. London: Verso, 1983.

Arberry, A. J., ed. *Persian Poems: An Anthology of Verse Translation*. London: J. M. Dent, 1954.

Bastide, Roger. "The Other Quilombo." *Maroon Societies: Rebel Slave Communities in the Americas*. Ed. Richard Price. 2nd ed. Baltimore: Johns Hopkins UP, 1979. 191–201.

Baudrillard, Jean. *Simulations*. Trans. Paul Foss, Paul Patton, and Philip Beitchman, New York: Semiotext(e), 1983.

Beeman, William. "Images of the Great Satan: Representations of the United States in the Iranian Revolution." *Religion and Politics in Iran: Shi'ism from Quietism to Revolution*. Ed. Nikki R. Keddie. New Haven: Yale UP, 1983. 191–217.

Bourdieu, Pierre. *Distinction: A Social Critique of the Judgment of Taste*. Trans. Richard Nice. Cambridge: Harvard UP, 1984.

———. *Outline of a Theory of Practice*. Trans. Richard Nice. New York: Cambridge UP, 1977.

Carpenter, Richard. "Ritual, Aesthetics, and TV." *Mass Media and Mass Man*. Ed. Alan Casty. 2d ed. New York: Holt, 1973. 134–42.

Cohen, Anthony P. *The Symbolic Construction of Community*. London: Tavistock, 1985.

Cottam, Richard. *Nationalism in Iran*. Pittsburgh: U of Pittsburgh P, 1979.

Dasenbrock, Reed Way. "Creating a Past: Achebe, Naipaul, Soyinka, Farah." *Salmagundi* 68–69 (Fall-Winter 1985–86): 312–32.

Gallop, Jane. *Reading Lacan*. Ithaca: Cornell UP, 1985.

Gans, Herbert J. *Popular Culture and High Culture: An Analysis and Evaluation of Taste*. New York: Basic, 1974.

Geertz, Clifford. *The Interpretation of Cultures*. New York: Basic, 1973.

Gellner, Ernest. *Nations and Nationalism*. London: Blackwell, 1987.

Good, Byron J., Mary-Jo DelVecchio Good, and Robert Moradi. "The Interpretation of Iranian Depressive Illness and Dysphoric Affect." *Culture and Depression: Studies in the Anthropology and Cross-Cultural Psychiatry of Affect and Disorder*. Ed. Arthur Kleinman and Byron Good. Berkeley: U of California P, 1985. 369–428.

Hall, Stuart. "Cultural Identity and Cinematic Representation." *Framework* 36 (1989): 68–81.

Hobsbawm, Eric. "Introduction: Inventing Traditions." *The Invention of Tradition*. Ed. Hobsbawm and Terence Ranger. Cambridge: Cambridge UP, 1983. 1–14.

301

Jameson, Fredric. "Postmodernism and Consumer Society." *The Anti-Aesthetic: Essays on Postmodern Culture.* Ed. Hal Foster. Port Townsend, WA: Bay P, 1983. 111–25.

Masson, J. M. *The Oceanic Feeling: The Origins of Religious Sentiment in Ancient India.* Dorrecht, Netherlands: Reidel, 1980.

Milani, Farzaneh. 1368. "Zadgah." *Par* 43 (1989): 26.

Morgan, Anne. "Interview: Shirazeh Hushiari." *Art Papers* 13.6 (1989): 14–17.

Myerhoff, Barbara. *Number Our Days.* New York: Touchstone, 1978.

Naderpour, Nader. 1365. "Gorbat-e She'r va She'r-e Ghorbat." *Rahavard* 3.11–12 (Summer and Fall 1986): 22–24.

Naficy, Hamid. "Iranian Writers, The Iranian Cinema, and the Case of *Dash Akol.*" *Iranian Studies* 18.2–4 (Spring-Autumn 1985): 231–51.

———. *Iran Media Index.* Westport, CT: Greenwood P, 1984.

———. "Televisual Fetishization in Exile." *Quarterly Review of Film and Video* 13. 1–3 (1991): 85–116.

Rachlin, Nahid. *Foreigner.* New York: Norton, 1978.

Rushdie, Salman. *The Satanic Verses.* New York: Viking, 1988.

Said, Edward. "The Mind in Winter: Reflections on Life in Exile." *Harpers'* (September 1984): 49–55.

———. *Orientalism.* New York: Vintage, 1979.

Schlesinger, Philip. "On National Identity: Some Conceptions and Misconceptions Criticized." *Social Science Information* 26.2 (1987): 219–64.

Stewart, Kathleen. "Nostalgia—A Polemic." *Cultural Anthropology* 3.3 (August 1988): 227–41.

Stewart, Susan. *On Longing: Narratives of the Miniature, the Gigantic, the Souvenir, the Collection.* Baltimore: Johns Hopkins UP, 1984.

Suhrawardi, Shihabuddin Yahya. "A Tale of Occidental Exile." *The Mystical and Visionary Treatises of Shihabuddin Yahya Suhrawardi.* Trans. W. M. Thackston, Jr. London: Octagon P, 1982. 100–108.

Turner, Victor. *Dramas, Fields, and Metaphors: Symbolic Action in Human Society.* Ithaca: Cornell UP, 1974.

———. *The Forest of Symbols: Aspects of Ndembu Ritual.* Ithaca: Cornell UP, 1967.

Culture, Ethnicity, and the Politics/Poetics of Representation

Gillian Bottomley
Macquarie University, Australia

1. The Study of Culture and Ethnicity

I will trace several interconnected themes in this essay, which can be stated separately at this stage. They are:

(1) to relate ideas, beliefs, and practices to formulations of ethnicity, that is, to separate the concepts of culture and ethnicity while recognizing their close kinship;

(2) to discuss relations of power in cultural processes, especially in forms of representation, of which ethnicity is one;

(3) to suggest a more anthropological approach to cultural studies, which tend to be mostly concerned with cultural products—literature, films, television programs—frequently read as texts without adequate contexts;

(4) to review some recent discussions about the cultural construction of identities and subjectivities in relation to discourses of gender, ethnicity, race, class, and culture; and

(5) to draw these threads together in a brief discussion of black music (through the work of Paul Gilroy) and of Greek music and dance, with particular reference to the politics and poetics of representation.

The conceptual framework linking these themes is a version of Bourdieu's constructivist structuralism, in which habitus, that is, "the embodiment of history," traces a dialectical relationship between structured circumstances and people's actions and perceptions. A close examination of the interaction between habitus and specific social fields, or terrains of struggle, can reveal positions of power that appear as natural, that support and sustain the attempt to delineate identities as natural and homogeneous. Bourdieu's concepts can also help to overcome the opposition of subjectivism/objectivism and to direct attention toward the interaction between these two. His emphasis on symbolic and cultural capital and on the struggle for symbolic power provides a dynamic alternative to overly materialist interpretations of cultural practices as epiphenomenal, as well as to reifications of tradition, ethnicity, community, and related boundary markers. Culture, therefore, can be seen not only as expressive, but also as constitutive, of social relations; its role in the definition of what is deemed necessary or even thinkable and in the reproduction of communality through practices and dispositions become visible within Bourdieu's formulation. Such visibility, in turn, illustrates the shortcomings of regarding culture as only the sum of articulated rules, traditions, and ideologies. This essay will discuss the cultural construction of several forms of power relations and communality, while attempting to cut across some of the essentialisms and assumptions of homogeneity implicit in discussions of culture, ethnicity, race, community, and the politics of identity.

In *Keywords* and *Culture,* Raymond Williams describes the concept of culture as one of the most difficult in the language. He traces a brief history of the concept from its early use as a noun of process—still found in words such as *horticulture* and *agriculture*—to a noun of configuration or generalization, a kind of informing spirit of a whole way of life, manifest in all social activities but especially in language, styles of art, and intellectual work. This is the sense taken up by anthropologists, who have examined the interconnectedness of social activities. However, this holistic approach tends to support a rather static view of cultures as integrated and enduring wholes that could clash on contact. Despite extensive debates and refinements within anthropology, this notion of culture as a whole way of life demarcated by tenaciously guarded traditions continues to be regarded by nonspecialists as the anthropological view of culture. In fact, anthropology, more than any other discipline, provides abundant evidence of the historical specificity and fluidity of cultural practices and beliefs, even as it retains the centrality of culture and the stress on interconnectedness. Yet as James Clifford, discussing the links between art, culture, and nineteenth century humanism, concludes, "[a] powerful structure of feeling continues to see culture, wherever it is found, as a coherent body that lives and dies. Culture is [seen as] enduring, traditional, structural (rather than contingent, syncretic, historical)" (235).

The persistence of this stubborn misconception of culture is complicated by the fact that anthropology has also been intermeshed with the development of nationalisms and the coupling of culture with ethnicity (Herzfeld, *Anthropology*). The idea that cultures exist as separate and integral entities clearly supported the project of defining the imagined communities of nations struggling for independence or dominance. In this process, culture became inextricably identified with ethnicity, as it still remains in most discussions of multiculturalism and cultural diversity. Before turning to the question of ethnicity, it is appropriate to state here that, in the definition I use, culture is a "constitutive social process" (following Williams, *Marxism*) that includes "*both* the meanings and values which" develop from "given historical conditions and relationships, through which (people) handle and respond to the conditions of existence; *and* the lived traditions and practices through which those understandings are expressed and in which they are embodied" (Hall "Cultural Studies" 26). These meanings, values, traditions, and practices can, therefore, arise from, express, and constitute a range of social relations, including those based on gender, class, and region of origin, or religion, as well as ethnicity. The conflation of culture with ethnicity gives rise to unitary categories such as Italian or Greek or Vietnamese or Pakistani cultures, used without further analysis, despite obvious complexities of regional, class, gender, historical, and social differences within such categories. This is particularly true of studies in political economy that turn to labor migration; they share with other economistic approaches a neglect of cultural practices and beliefs, which are viewed as ideological or at best epiphenomenal to the real issues.[1] Some of those opposing the political economists have reacted by asserting the primordiality of ethnic consciousness or the primacy of ethnic identification over class affiliation (see Glazer and Moynihan for extensive discussions of these positions). Ironically, these politically opposed positions have a point of convergence in regarding culture/ethnicity as unproblematic because already constituted. The real opposition here is between a pluralist position that regards ethnic minorities as legitimate pressure groups and a critique of the very assumptions on which pluralism is based, particularly those that take access and equity for granted (see Martin, "Development" and "Multiculturalism," for discussions of these assumptions in Australian multiculturalism).

Recently, both of these political positions have been challenged and, to some extent, overtaken by critiques arising from several directions, including feminists, postcolonial writers, and others who object to the notion that, in Marx's words, they could not represent themselves, but "must be represented." I will discuss some of these critiques in more detail later, but I mention them here in order to stress the significance of the ways in which they call into question the dominant paradigms of culture and society, as well as of the constitution of knowledge about both of these concepts. Most importantly, these critiques have demonstrated that categories and ways of knowing do not simply or naturally develop from innate predispositions, but rather are constructed within relations of power and maintained, reproduced, and resisted in specific and sometimes contradictory ways. Analyses of this kind often stress the intersection and intermeshing of dimensions such as ethnicity, class, gender, and cultural practices (see Anthias and Yuval-Davis; and Bottomley, de Lepervanche, and Martin).

Of course, critiques of grand narratives—including those of nations, culture, or ethnicity—and the construction of metanarratives and counternarratives are neither recent in origin nor necessarily postmodern. Hegemony has long been resisted, contested, and undermined (for accounts of early examples of such contestation, see Hobsbawm's *Primitive Rebels* and Lanternari's *Religions of the Oppressed*). Yet surprisingly, various modernist hegemonies have had relative success in controlling resistance. It is this success that makes the question of culture so important, particularly if we are to try to understand what Foucault described as subjection, the process whereby people subjugate themselves even as their subjectivity takes shape. The mechanisms of subjection need to be studied in relation to mechanisms of exploitation and domination, but "they do not merely constitute the 'terminals' of more fundamental mechanisms. They entertain complex and circular relations with other forms" (Foucault 213).

In an important essay entitled "Cultural Studies: Two Paradigms," Stuart Hall discusses the work of "culturalists" such as Williams and Thompson, the "structuralisms" of Lévi-Strauss and Althusser, and, reflecting on Gramsci and the radical heterogeneity of Foucault, some articulation of these ways of understanding what he described as "the dialectic between conditions and consciousness" (36). Hall's work has been influential in some of the most sophisticated studies of immigration, racism, and polyethnicity, such as *Policing the Crisis* and *The Empire Strikes Back* (both from the Birmingham Centre for Contemporary Cultural Studies) and Paul Gilroy's *There Ain't No Black in the Union Jack*.

2. Constructivist Structuralism: Pierre Bourdieu

Before discussing some of the more recent work of Hall and Gilroy, I will elaborate further on the "contructivist structuralism" of Pierre Bourdieu, who argues, first against a subjectivism that privileges lived experience and fails to scrutinize the theoretical and social conditions within which practical knowledge is developed; and second, against an objectivism that grasps practices from outside and obscures the fact that "the truth of social interaction is never entirely in the interaction as observed" (*Choses Dites* 153). According to Bourdieu, subjectivism reduces structure to interaction and objectivism deduces actions and interactions from structure while assuming the existence of unified groups and the homogeneity of conditions. Both perspectives are necessary, but social scientists must also recognize that social reality is an object of perceptions, including their own, developed within specific constraints.

I noted earlier that Bourdieu's concept of habitus offers a way through the separation of subjective and objective. Habitus is the process whereby those who occupy similar positions in social and historical space come to share a certain "sense of place" and develop categories of perception that provide a commonsense understanding of the world, especially of what is natural, plausible, or even imaginable. These categories, however, are socially produced within specific contexts, and they continue to mediate the experience and interpretation of changing objective conditions. Thus, the durable, transposable dispositions so central to the acquisition of habitus in childhood are overlaid and transformed by adjustment to later circumstances. Yet those adjustments are themselves biased by preexisting perceptions that mostly operate below the level of consciousness. Habitus is not determining, but it is a powerful mediating construct that can predefine what is necessary or thinkable.

Because the concept of habitus implies a continuing interaction between circumstances, actions, and perceptions, it requires a break with some revered dualisms, such as determinism versus freedom, conditioning versus creativity, individual versus society, and interior versus exterior (the latter is particularly important in ideas about the body). Habitus manifests itself in practice, in action and movement, in the way one orients oneself in relation to specific social fields. For example, habitus usually forms the basis of personal relationships and what is described as homogamy, whereby people tend to marry partners with similar backgrounds. As Bourdieu demonstrates clearly in *Distinction,* habitus can also provide a form of cultural and symbolic capital in itself, as is the case with the "natural" ease and grace of those "born to rule."

The notion of habitus seems particularly pertinent to a consideration of the ways in which constructions such as gender, class, ethnicity, and race become literally "embodied knowledges," operating largely below the level of consciousness. Habitus mediates between positions and practices, so that relations of power appear as natural. This stress on the embodiment of power relations below the level of consciousness and language has been described by Bourdieu as requiring a kind of psychosocioanalysis. In a recent discussion with Terry Eagleton, he commented that "the work of emancipation is as much a form of gymnastics as consciousness-raising" ("Discussion"). At the same meeting, he described Marxism as "too Cartesian, too much concerned with consciousness." His own work demonstrates how, in his words, "the social world operates in terms of *practices,"* the result of interaction between habitus and specific social fields. Both social field and habitus are products of history; each is dynamic and a terrain of struggle that can only be delineated through a combination of historical and ethnographic analysis.

In his stress on the structural properties of social fields, Bourdieu appears to provide the precise articulation Hall seeks when he claims that what has been missing in cultural studies is analytic work that is structural, historical, and ethnographic. In fact, the issue of *Media, Culture and Society* following that in which Hall's essay ("Cultural Studies") was first published took up Bourdieu's work as "one of the most promising attempts to think forwards from Hall's two paradigms" of culturalism and structuralism (Garnham and Williams 1). In this issue, Nicholas Garnham and Raymond Williams carefully analyze Bourdieu's work on cultural appropriation and symbolic power but fail to address his emphasis on reflexivity and the position of the researcher in relation to his or her research. The authors refer to Bourdieu's criticism of subjectivism (which they construe as phenomenology, characteristic of studies in which the observer is also a participant) and of objectivism (a tendency to fetishize structures and render people mere performers or bearers of structures). Garnham and Williams attribute this latter tendency to anthropologists in particular, but Bourdieu's net is wider and includes sociological attempts to use ethnographic method. In *Distinction,* for example, he criticizes those who claim to describe working class experience when they are in fact describing their own relation to that experience. Furthermore, Bourdieu's theory of practice includes a theory of intellectual practice, whereby both observer and observed are subject to critical analysis. His ideas on this topic were formulated largely in relation to questions of authentic or legitimate knowledge and the struggle for symbolic power, the central struggle of intellectuals. Those who claim to represent others also create representations and categories—the latter being a word, as Bourdieu points out, that derives from the Greek verb "to accuse publicly" (*Choses Dites* 39).

3. Identities, Ethnicities, and Representations

This discussion brings us back to issues of ethnicity and representation. I remarked earlier that the conflation of culture and ethnicity had privileged a form of categorizing that emphasizes ethnic constructs at the expense of other cultural practices, for example, those that generate the embodiment of gender and class relations. This observation has been made mostly within the context of arguments about structured inequalities, where it can lead to a debate about competing claims and hierarchies of oppression (see Anthias and Yuval-Davis, and Parmar). The process often reinforces essentialisms and categories as contenders argue on behalf of women, blacks, ethnics, or the working class, each seen by its champions as being more oppressed than other unitary categories. One outcome of this form of identity politics can be a retreat to separate "ghettoised lifestyles" (Parmar). Another, described by Said, is the development of an excluding insider mentality whereby only those who are insiders by virtue of experience or by virtue of method, possess the correct form of knowledge and can write about certain subjects. In this process, differences are reified into impenetrable boundaries. Moreover, the dualistic approach of a unitary Us versus a unitary Them continues to mystify the interpenetration and intermeshing of the powerful constructs of race, class, and gender and to weaken attempts at reflexivity. It also raises crucial questions about representation, both in the political sense of who speaks on behalf of others, and in the wider sense of how these others are being presented, or re-presented. Admittedly, the politics of identity have sometimes empowered and strenghened, providing a space within which people excluded from various grand narratives have been able to recognize themselves and to analyze and contest some of those narratives. But, as Bourdieu's constructivist structuralism suggests, both the subjective and objective dimensions of even their experience need to be addressed, as well as the thorny issue of the extent to which observers remain within the discourses they seek to criticize.

The issue of representation has been central to more recent analyses of ethnicities, identities, and the constitution of subjectivities. Hall describes representation as "an extremely slippery customer" ("New Ethnicities" 27). But he also argues that because events, relations, and structures can only be constructed within a discourse, "the scenarios of representation—subjectivity, identity, politics— [have] a formative, not merely an expressive place in the construction of social and political life" ("New Ethnicities" 27).

In a book coedited by Hall, Rosalind Brunt discusses the politics of identity, claiming representation as her starting point. Brunt's notion of a "set of identities" to which we are assigned at birth (based on color, gender, class, nationality, kinship) bears some resemblance to Bourdieu's habitus,[2] and Brunt also refers to Gramsci's injunction that self-knowledge means knowing oneself as "a product of the historical process to date, which has deposited in you an infinity of traces without leaving an inventory" (qtd. in Brunt 154). Bourdieu goes further, to consider the crisscrossing of traces as a continuous process. One of the most interesting points of Brunt's essay, however, is her account of the challenge to the subjective/ objective dichotomy that arose from feminist politics. Feminist activists, she argues, often speak from their own experience, thus putting themselves within the frame of political involvement and challenging the supposed homogeneities of various political categories. Although feminism is no unitary category either, Brunt's central point here problematizes representation, underscoring the need to recognize that identity is often based on an assumption of homogeneity and that relations of power operate horizontally as well as vertically, internally as well as externally. Her conclusions are that homogeneity cannot be a basis for unity but that unity must come from "a whole variety of heterogeneous, possibly antagonistic, maybe magnificently diverse, identities and circumstances" (158). A less celebratory version of this point is seen in Fraser and Nicholson's plea for a theoretical counterpart of the sort of feminist solidarity "essential for overcoming the oppression of women in its endless variety and monotonous similarity" (391).

From a different direction, these conclusions echo Hall's claim that "it is an immensely important gain when we recognise that all identity is constructed across difference and begin to live with the politics of difference" ("Minimal Selves" 45). Hall links this project to that of the new conceptions of ethnicity being constructed "as a kind of counter to the old discourses of nationalism or national identity" ("Minimal Selves" 46). He goes on to warn that ethnicity "can be a constitutive element in the most viciously regressive kind of nationalism or national identity" (46), but it can also focus attention on specificities, on the fact that personal identity is formed at the unstable point "where the unspeakable stories of subjectivities meet the narratives of history, of a culture" (44).

His more recent essay about new ethnicities and the politics of representation signals the end of essentialism and a need to understand that, for example, "the central issues of race always appear historically . . . and are crossed and recrossed by the categories of class, of gender and ethnicity" ("New Ethnicities" 28). Hall points out that black politics is often silent on questions of sexuality and class, an observation that can be applied, in modified form, to any unidimensional and essentialist politics that ignores the interweaving of gender, ethnicity, and class.

Interestingly, Hall also suggests that the concept of ethnicity should be disarticulated from its position in the discourse of multiculturalism and transcoded. He argues that "[i]f the black subject and black experience are not stabilised by Nature or by some other essential guarantee, then it must be the case that they are constructed historically, culturally, politically—and the concept which refers to this is 'ethnicity'" ("New ethnicities" 29). This term, therefore, acknowledges the specificity of subjectivities and the contextual bases of knowledge, including those that are presented as nonethnic, such as the embattled, hegemonic conception of Englishness contested in *Policing the Crisis* and *The Empire Strikes Back*. To develop a positive conception of the ethnicity of the margins, Hall advocates a separation of the concept of ethnicity from those of nation or race.

Hall's essay on new ethnicities was written in the context of a discussion of black film in British cinema. The view of culture found in his essay, therefore, varies slightly from the definition I quoted earlier, and emphasizes practices of music, literature, and cinema that challenge dominant aesthetic discourses, contesting marginalization and stereotypes. These oppositional perspectives have called into question the idea of a coherent national identity, as well as the representation of blacks as inevitably problems or victims. Films like *Dreaming Rivers, Playing Away,* and *My Beautiful Laundrette* have also revealed the variety and fragmentation of British life, and the fact that identity—and habitus—are constructed across such differences. We must keep in mind, however, that access to funding often accompanies further pressures toward homogenization, as cultural workers are presumed to represent an entire community. This is an important issue in countries like Britain, Canada, and Australia, where official policies of multiculturalism legitimate particular definitions of ethnic culture.

4. Constructing Ethnicities: Culture, Multiculturalism, and Communality

The concept of community, like that of culture, is spiked with historical and political symbolism. Politicians, journalists, and self-elected representatives of all kinds refer to such imagined constituencies as the local community, the gay community, or the Muslim, Aboriginal, Greek, or Italian communities; indeed, they even refer to the entire electorate as the community. This is untenable from an anthropological perspective, which regards a community as marked by face-to-face interaction, multiplex ties, and shared common values. The usages referred to above may cover people with some shared values, but the status of these imagined communities often rests most firmly in the homogenizing intentions of the observer. Nevertheless, one of the most impressive commentators on ethnicity, racism, and what he calls "the dialectics of diaspora identification," Paul Gilroy, has continued to stress the political significance of interpretive communities that recognize difference as well as similarity. In Gilroy's usage, the symbolic aspects of community enable people to act socially and cohesively in the absence of structures provided by formal organizations. Gilroy is acutely aware of the dangers of homogenization, as well as the difficulties of steering between the Scylla of mystical particularism and the Charybdis of celebratory pluralism. The first course can be fueled by multiculturalism and the structures of funding and legitimation; the second can result in a denial of the specifically racialized forms of power and subordination. In Gilroy's words, "the critical political project forged in the journey from slave ship to citizenship is in danger of being wrecked by the seemingly insoluble conflict between two distinct but currently symbiotic perspectives" ("It Ain't" 1, 4–5). Moreover, claims to purity and difference and "a hermetically sealed culture" can actually mirror some of the claims of the racists of the so-called New Right. They also cover with a cloak of silence embarrassing internal divisions based on class, gender, and sexuality.

Gilroy breaks that silence by reference to black musical expression. He believes that the vitality and complexity of black music offer a way through the oppositions of essentialism versus pluralism and tradition versus modernity and argues that black music presents a "politics of transfiguration" that refuses to accept the modernist/rationalist separation of politics from morality and ethics. It evokes a politics of fulfillment, immanent within modernity, "created under the nose of the overseer," existing on "a lower frequency where it is played, danced and acted as well as sung about" ("It Ain't" 1, 11). Unsurprisingly, this critical tradition seeks emancipation not through work but through a form of poetics. I cannot do justice here to Gilroy's detailed and highly skilled exposition, but I will note several points of particular relevance to my argument. One is that this musical culture "supplies a great deal of the courage required to go on living in the present" ("It Ain't 10), not by denying the racial terror of slavery and its aftermath but by developing a (partly hidden) critique of some of the grand narratives of modernity. This subculture is not "the intuitive expression of some racial essence, but is in fact an elementary historical acquisition" (Gilroy, "It Ain't" 1, 13).

Gilroy borrows from Richard Wright, who borrowed from Nietzsche, a notion of "the frog's perspective" as one that entails a double vision. In Gilroy's formulation, the ethico-political problems of "what counts as history and as reality . . . have been the substance of black expressive culture since slavery, . . . from the time we walked through the door of Christianity and became people of the West (in it but not organically of it)" ("Cruciality" 41). This double vision developed in dialogue with high modernity and made possible an ethics grounded in the contradictions between, on the one hand, the modernist message of rationality and freedom and, on the other, the experience of slavery and racial oppression. It is Gilroy's contention that "the history of black music enables us to trace something of the means through which the unity of ethics and politics has been reproduced as a form of folk knowledge" ("It Ain't" 91, 13).

The main formal feature of these musical traditions is antiphony, call and response, which blurs the self/other distinction, as foregrounded, for example, in improvised jazz solos, where a single performer, backed and supported by the group, creates within an explicitly referential tradition. Gilroy argues that the practice of antiphony anticipates new and nondominating forms of social relations. As a longtime observer of jazz, I would state the case more strongly, in terms of a rehearsal and enactment of a potentially liberating form of exchange, especially among musicians, but also between musicians and audience.

Gilroy's analysis is not confined to jazz, but the international trajectory of jazz serves as a metaphor for his shift in focus away from the colonizing center toward "the web of black Atlantic political culture" ("It Ain't" 15). Gilroy's work provides rich analyses of the embodiment and cultural representation of specific historical and political circumstances. In these analyses, England is a particular location, seen from the perspective of a black diaspora (see Gilroy, *There Ain't No Black in the Union Jack* and "Cruciality and the Frog's Perspective").

This shift is important, first, in redefining a specific context as one among a range of possibilities, and second, in allowing for some understanding of the scope of such vast cultural networks. The attention paid to minorities within countries of immigration, on the one hand, and to global capital, on the other, often obscures the human and cultural links between these two, the international networks based on kinship, friendship, and shared ethnicities and the highly sophisticated cultural forms that flow through and sustain those networks.

5. Case in Point: The Greek Diaspora

For the last 20 years or so, I have maintained an internationalist, network-based approach to the study of migration and the "politics and poetics of culture" with particular reference to Greek Australians. My studies have included comparisons of cultural and social forms such as gender relations, dowry, dance, and music in Greece and among Australians of Greek origin.[3] The specific transformations and renegotiation of practices such as these provide, as Gilroy suggests, a kind of "frog's perspective" on societies of immigration, a view of the ways in which a particular context can both develop and truncate the life chances of immigrants and their offspring. At the same time, diasporic identifications offer dynamic countercultures to those in which immigrants are only factory workers, slaves, "wogs," or unwanted foreigners. These countercultures have spatial and temporal dimensions that can dwarf those of any immigrant-receiving country.

Salman Rushdie recently commented that we live in the century of the migrant, as well as that of the Bomb. Actually, it is increasingly becoming the century of the refugee, but migration, forced and unforced, has already created a world of diasporas. The sense of double or multiple consciousness generated by the experience of relative marginality can cut across the dichotomies of subjectivity versus objectivity as well as those of private versus public and individual versus collective. As we have seen, the habitus generated by a radical movement from one set of circumstances to another has particular spatial and temporal dimensions. Moreover, as Gilroy and others have demonstrated, there are countermemories threaded throughout the cultural experience of those who are not masters or guardians of the grand narratives (or even players in what Bourdieu calls "the main games"). These countermemories can be traced in art, in oral traditions, in partly submerged forms of knowledge that are not the legitimated knowledges of those in authority. Lipsitz has persuasively linked this notion of counter-memory to Kristeva's essay on "women's time," which compares cursive time, the time of linear history, to monumental time, the time of life cycles and private rituals. Lipsitz argues that countermemory acts within the limits of historical time while retaining and celebrating the divergent and even oppositional practices of monumental time (see Lipsitz, esp. 229). Countermemories can, therefore, form elements of a counterculture, a base for resistance and a space defined across difference. Most importantly, they encourage a kind of intertextuality, a way of viewing the past within the categories of the present, not as some uninterrupted continuity, but including disjunctions, conflicts, and what I have elsewhere called "muted modes," not fully articulated but expressed in forms such as the antiphony of black music, as described by Gilroy.

My own study of muted modes and the politics of culture has been partly concerned with Greek music and dance, and I want to trace some of the themes of the discussion so far with reference to Greek dance.[4] My perspective is historical and ethnographic, touching on the interweaving of gender/sexuality, ethnicity, and other relations of power in dance, as well as aspects of folkloricizing and the constitution of personal and communal identity in the Greek diaspora.

Music and dance are important themes in Greek sociality. In her wonderful study, *Dance and the Body Politic in Northern Greece*, Jane Cowan comments that dance in Greece involves both social knowledge and social power. Her book explores definitions of the imaginable through dance events that, she argues, "can be read as an embodied discourse on the moral relations between the individual and the larger collectivity" (131). In the celebrations she describes, elements of social inequality and social affiliation are "bound together on the topography of the body . . . within an event that is vivid, intoxicating, engrossing" (133). Cowan's work is important in its critique of monolithic notions about a unitary and shared culture, in its emphasis on contestations and ambivalences, and for its demonstration of the social and historical constitution of habitus, the embodiment of history.

In Australian critiques of multiculturalism, ethnic dance has been summarily dismissed as trivial and folkloric, as partly responsible for an image of a perpetually singing, dancing ethnic that denies the harsh realities of racialized forms of exploitations and exclusion. These criticisms have considerable weight, as we have already seen in the context of the celebratory pluralism discussed above. But music and dance are not merely folkloric—nor, for that matter, is the folkloric constructed only within countries of immigration. In Greece, for example, the concept of the folk was developed in the post-Ottoman period along with the development of nationalism (see Giannaris and Herzfeld, *Ours Once More*). Folklore studies—*laografia*—had the intention of constructing imagined communities among the majority of the population, the rural people, who had been influenced by hundreds of years of Byzantine and Ottoman rule but were to be incorporated within the scope of the new nationalism as bearers of ancient traditions, and therefore as deserving the support of European philhellenes such as Byron, who found "barbarous and oriental traits" among the existing inhabitants of the "cradle of Western civilization" (Marchand 94). As Herzfeld's later work explains, the identification with Hellenism is ambivalent and at times resisted (see "Within"), but my point here is that folkloric representations have been a familiar aspect of the politics of culture in Greece, as in other countries. As such, they have generated forms of resistance or at least skepticism. Alkis Raftis, an expert on traditional music and dance, once commented to me that "if you hear only folk music on the radio, you know there's been a coup."

This raises another aspect of dance and music in relation to politics. I have argued elsewhere that authoritarian regimes everywhere have always attempted to control music and dance (Bottomley, "Cultures"). Jacques Attali, in his study of music, describes thirteenth and fourteenth century prohibitions on dancing in churches and "assemblies of women, for the purpose of dancing and singing," near cemeteries and other sacred places. Anyone performing dances before the churches of the saints could be subjected to three years of penance (Attali 22). Most of what is known about dance during the Byzantine era (fifth to fifteenth centuries) "comes from the prohibitions and exhortations of the Orthodox Church" (Raftis 1). The cultural revolution in China, General Pinochet's regime in Chile, and the colonels[7] in Greece provide further examples of the punishment and restriction of musicians and other artists who failed to toe the correct line. Nevertheless, medieval Christians continued to dance, Chinese musicians continued to play, and Chilean and Greek composers and performers were highly influential in generating opposition to their oppressive regimes (see Bottomley, "Cultures"). Part of the force of music and dance is that they cannot be readily contained within authorized forms of knowledge; they are, in large part, communicated below the level of consciousness.

Carnival-type presentations often serve to underscore ethnic stereotypes. But Greek dance, despite its association with important rituals such as weddings and post-Easter celebrations, is much more than just an acting out of some timeless tradition or an unquestioned communality. Oppositions and ambivalences also arise in dance events. Cowan's work, for example, describes the celebration

315

of the gendered order in such instances as male appropriation of public space and ostentatious payment of musicians. The ambivalence of female sexuality as both pleasurable and threatening gains special force in dance events. There is also a particular tension between the ideas of the collectivity in *kefi,* a state of heightened communal sociability, and the possibility of subversion by someone who makes his own kefi too forcefully, thus disrupting the collective experience.

The politics of interpersonal relations and the politics of status hierarchies in Greek dance are transformed in the diaspora because the social field is different. But some of these differences can be explored in detail precisely through closer attention to practices such as music and dance. Young Greek-Australian women, for example, dance with great enthusiasm the *tsamiko,* formerly a male dance closely identified with the fiercely moustachioed mountain guerrillas who fought the war of independence against the Ottoman Empire. Male dance teachers cheerfully assist their female students in mastering the athletic leaps that traditionally demonstrated the virility of male dancers. Women also perform the (usually male) solo dance *zebekiko* and launch into the rather orientalist *tsifteteli,* a form of belly dance, with a robust sensuality that conveys little ambivalence about either the sensuality or the orientalism. Lately, Latin American dance fashions have appeared in some variants of these dances. These are obviously spontaneous adaptations, but they reflect something of the changes in modes of sensuality and the embodiment of gender relations (both of which are also changing in Greece, of course). More formal examples of transformations are syncretic dances such as the *Zorba,* developed by dance teachers to pick up on the popularity of the Zorba image and the semicircular *syrtaki,* a composite dance loved by tourists and disdained by dance purists.

These dances may serve to objectify Greekness, not only to the homogenized Anglo Other of critical parlance, but to Greeks as well. As Attali has warned, this process can signal a strategy of domination. He notes three such strategies with regard to music. The first is in ritual, to make people forget about generalized violence; the second is in representation, to make them believe in the harmony of the world; and the third is in repetition, to silence and control. In Attali's words, "[f]etishized as a commodity, music is illustrative of the evolution of our entire society: deritualize a social form, repress an activity of the body, specialize its practice, sell it as a spectacle, generalize its consumption, then see to it that it is stockpiled until it loses its meaning" (Attali 5).

All these elements are present in Greek dance, which conveys a model of collective harmony (up to a point) and is often fetishized as a commodity and sold as spectacle (the latter especially, but not only, in multicultural carnival-type performances, in Greece itself as well as in the diaspora). However, as we have seen, Greek dance and music can also subvert these strategies. They developed in step with political resistance of all kinds, from the tsamiko of the independence fighters through the *rembetika* songs of the Piraeus hashish joints to the stirring music of Theodorakis and Markopoulos. At a less portentous level, the forms of Greek music and dance also contain different communicative modes, comparable to those discussed by Gilroy—for example, the call and response of musicians, between musicians and dancers, and between dancers themselves. The notion of kefi, as noted earlier, symbolizes both the experience and the fragility of collectivity. Greek-Australians also consciously make positive distinctions between the sensuality and expressiveness of Greek music and dance and the more alienated and individualistic Anglo-Australian forms of sociality. This is not simply perceiving oneself as a singing, dancing ethnic but is marking a certain deficit in the dominant forms of ethnic expression. It can also lead to an ironic assessment of both forms, precisely the double (or multiple) consciousness I mentioned earlier that reflects very accurately the complexity of the context and comes very close to Bourdieu's reflexive ethnography. Migration and the experience of living across difference can bring into crisis the taken-for-granted assumptions that form the basis of the logic of practice. Such practices are not readily amenable to verbal analysis, but Cowan's and Gilroy's studies demonstrate the fruitfulness of concentrating on what Bourdieu calls the logic of practice. Not only does this entail the objectification of subjectivity and the subjectification of the objective, it also requires that the presuppositions inherent in the position of the observer be called into question (see Bourdieu, *The Logic of Practice*).

A detailed study of the logic of these particular practices is not possible within the limits of this essay. My intention here has been to provide some understanding of what Hall has described as "that unstable point where the unspeakable stories of subjectivities" meet, contest, reproduce, and transform the narratives of history and culture ("Minimal Selves" 44). Culture both constitutes and is constituted by social relations, in defining what is deemed necessary or thinkable and in reproducing communality through practices, dispositions, and habitus.

Notes

1. Notable exceptions to this generalization can be found in the work of Robert Miles, Annie Phizacklea, and Michael Piore.

2. I recognize that I have elided some of the considerable differences between the theoretical frameworks of Hall, Gilroy, Brunt, and Bourdieu. It is especially important to note, in this

context, that class is central to the constitution of habitus. Nevertheless, Bourdieu has carefully pointed out that "a class or class fraction is defined not only by its position in the relations of production, as identified through indices such as occupation, income or even educational level, but also by a certain sex-ratio, a certain distribution in geographical space (which is never socially neutral) and by a whole set of subsidiary characteristics which may function, in the form of tacit requirements, as real principles of selection or exclusion without ever being formally stated (this is the case with ethnic origin and sex)" (*Distinction* 102).

3. See Bottomley, "Some Greek Sex Roles," "After the Odyssey," "Perpetuation," "Cultures," and "From Another Place"; and Bottomley and Raftis.

4. Greek music, dance, and lyrics are not easily separable and are usually created in close inter-relation.

Works Cited

Anthias, Floya, and Nira Yuval-Davis. "Contextualising Feminism: Gender, Ethnic and Class Divisions." *Feminist Review* 15 (1983): 62–75.

Attali, Jacques. *Noise: A Political Economy of Music*. Minneapolis: U of Minnesota P, 1985.

Bottomley, Gillian. *After the Odyssey: A Study of Greek Australians*. Brisbane: University of Queensland Press, 1979.

———. "Cultures, Multiculturalism and the Politics of Representation." *Journal of Intercultural Studies* 8.2 (1987): 1–10.

———. *From Another Place: Migration and the Politics of Culture*. Melbourne: Cambridge UP, 1992.

———. "Migration, Ageing and the Language of Dance." *Ethnographika*. Ed. Irene Loutzaki. Napflion: Peloponnesian Folklore Foundation, 1992.

———. "Perpétuation de la dot chez les Grecs d'Australie: Transformation et renégociation des pratiques traditionelles." *Familles et biens en Grèce et à Chypre*. Ed. Colette Piault. Paris:l'Harmattan, 1985.

———. "Some Greek Sex Roles: Ideals, Expectations and Action in Australia and Greece." *Australian and New Zealand Journal of Sociology* 10.1 (1974): 8–16.

———. "Towards a Sociology of Dance: Terpsichore and Other Greeks." *To Yiofiri*. Sydney: Dept. of Modern Greek, Univ. of Sydney, 1988.

Bottomley, Gillian, M. de Lepervanche, and J. Martin, eds. *Intersexions: Gender/Class/Culture/Ethnicity*. Sydney: Allen & Unwin, 1991.

Bottomley, Gillian, and Alkis Raftis. "Shared Tasks and Communal Celebrations in Rural Greece." *Journal of Intercultural Studies* 5.1 (1984): 22–23.

Bourdieu, Pierre. *Choses Dites*. Paris: Editions de Minuit, 1987.

———. Discussion with Terry Eagleton, Institute of Contemporary Arts, London, May 14, 1991.

———. *Distinction*. Trans. Richard Nice. London: Routledge Kegan Paul, 1986.

———. *The Logic of Practice*. Trans. Richard Nice. Cambridge: Polity Press, 1990.

———. *Outline of a Theory of Practice*. Trans. Richard Nice. Cambridge: Cambridge UP, 1977.

Brunt, Rosalind. "The Politics of Identity." *New Times*. Ed. Stuart Hall and M. Jacques. London: Lawrence and Wishart, 1989.

Clifford, James. "On Collecting Art and Culture." *The Predicament of Culture*. Ed. Clifford. Cambridge: Harvard UP, 1988.

Cowan, Jane. *Dance and the Body Politic in Northern Greece*. Princeton: Princeton UP, 1990.

Foucault, Michel. "The Subject and Power." Afterword. *Michel Foucault: Beyond Structuralism and Hermeneutics*. H. Dreyfus and P. Rabinow. Chicago: Harvester Press, University of Chicago, 1982.

Fraser, Nancy, and Linda Nicholson. "Social Criticism Without Philosophy: An Encounter Between Feminism and Postmodernism." *Theory, Culture and Society* 5 (1988): 373–94.

Garnham, Nicholas, and Raymond Williams. "Pierre Bourdieu and the Sociology of Culture: An Introduction." *Media, Culture and Society* 2 (1980): 209–223.

Giannaris, George. *Mikis Theodorakis: Music and Social Change*. London: George Allen & Unwin, 1973.

Gilroy, Paul. "Cruciality and the Frog's Perspective." *Third Text* 5 (Winter 1988–89): 33–44.

——. "It Ain't Where You're From, It's Where You're At . . . The Dialectics of Diasporic Identification." *Third Text* 13 (Winter 1990–91): 3–16.

——. "Nothing but Sweat Inside My Hand: Diaspora Aesthetics and Black Arts in Britain." *Black Film, British Cinema*. ICA Documents 7, 44–46. London: Institute of Contemporary Arts, 1988.

——. *There Ain't No Black in the Union Jack*. London: Hutchinson, 1987.

Glazer, Nathan, and Daniel Patrick Moynihan. *Ethnicity: Theory and Experience*. Cambridge: Harvard UP, 1975.

Hall, Stuart. "Cultural Studies: Two Paradigms." *Culture, Ideology and Social Process: A Reader*. Ed. T. Bennett, G. Martin, C. Mercer, and J. Woollacott. Milton Keynes, Eng.: Open UP, 1981.

——. "Minimal Selves" *Identity: The Real Me*. ICA Documents 6, 44–46. London: Institute of Contemporary Arts, 1987.

——. "New Ethnicities." *Black Film, British Cinema*. ICA Documents 7, 27–30. London: Institute of Contemporary Arts, 1988.

Hall, Stuart, et al., eds. *The Empire Strikes Back*. Centre for Contemporary Cultural Studies, Birmingham, Eng. London: Hutchinson, 1982.

——. *Policing the Crisis*. Centre for Contemporary Cultural Studies, Birmingham Eng. London: Macmillan, 1978.

Herzfeld, H. *Anthropology through the Looking Glass*. Cambridge: Cambridge UP, 1987.

——. *Ours Once More: Folklore, Ideology and the Making of Modern Greece*. Austin: U of Texas P, 1982.

——. "Within and Without: The Category of 'Female' in the Ethnography of Greece." *Gender and Power in Modern Greece*. Ed. Jill Dubisch.

Hobsbawm, Eric. *Primitive Rebels*. Manchester: Manchester UP, 1963.

Kristeva, Julia. "Women's Time. *The Kristeva Reader*. Ed. Toril Moi. New York: Columbia UP, 1986. 193–94.

Lanternari, Vittorio. *Religions of the Oppressed*. New York: Knopf, 1965.

Lipsitz, George. *Time Passages*. Minneapolis: U of Minnesota P, 1990.

Marchand, Leslie. *Byron: A Portrait*. London: Futura, 1970.

Martin, Jeannie. "Multiculturalism and Feminism." *Intersexions: Gender/Class/Culture/Ethnicity*. Ed. Gillian Bottomley, Marie de Lepervanche, and Jeannie Martin. Sydney: Allen & Unwin, 1991.

———. "The Development of Multiculturalism." *Report to the Minister for Immigration and Ethnic Affairs*. 2: 120–60 (Canberra: Aust. Govt. Printer), 1983.

Miles, Robert. *Racism*. London: Routledge, 1989.

Miles, Robert, and Annie Phizacklea. *Racism and Political Action in Britain*. London: Routledge Kegan Paul, 1979.

Parmar, Pratibha. "Other Kinds of Dreams." *Feminist Review* 31 (1989): 55–65.

Phizacklea, Annie, ed. *One Way Ticket*. London: Routledge Kegan Paul, 1983.

Piore, Michael. *Birds of Passage*. Cambridge: Cambridge UP, 1980.

Raftis, Alkis. *The World of Greek Dance*. Athens: Polytypo, 1985.

Rushdie, Salman, with Günter Grass. "Writing for a Future." *Voices: Writers and Politics*. Ed. B. Bourne, U. Eichler, and D. Herman. Nottingham: Spokesman and Hobo Press, 1987.

Said, Edward. "Orientalism Reconsidered" *Race and Class* 27.2 (1985): 1–15.

Williams, Raymond. *Culture*. Glasgow: Fontana, 1981.

———. *Keywords*. Glasgow: Fontana, 1976.

———. *Marxism and Literature*. London: Oxford UP, 1977.

"Like a Song Gone Silent": The Political Ecology of Barbarism and Civilization in *Waiting for the Barbarians* and *The Legend of the Thousand Bulls*

Arif Dirlik
Duke University

*Everything we ever knew about the movement of the sea was pre-
served in the verses of a song. For thousands of years we went where
we wanted and came home safe, because of the song. . . . There was
a song for goin' to China and a song for goin' to Japan, a song for the
big island and a song for the smaller one. All she had to know was
the song and she knew where she was. To get back, she just sang the
song in reverse. . . .*

Ann Cameron, *Daughters of Copper Woman*,
as quoted in Bruce Chatwin, *The Songlines*

Of all the ideas that have gone into shaping our conception of
history, those that are products of the juxtaposition of the civilized
against the barbarian are among the most fundamental, universal,
and persistent. History as we know it is the account of civilization
which, in this conception, is another way of saying a break with and
subsequent conquest of nature and the creation of a physical and
social space within which men (and to a lesser extent, women) can
overcome the animality of their natures to become human beings.
Outside that space is the realm of the barbarian: a realm without
history, a realm represented as that which civilization seeks not to
be and in which humanity is once again subject to nature and animality. While the boundaries of the two realms may shift and, with
them, our ideas of what it means to be civilized (and therefore
human), there is little disputing that the conflict between civilization and barbarism is a grand metahistorical theme around which
we have thought and written history.

Our very conception of civilization also predetermines what the
outcome of such conflict must be. The power of the concept is such
that it is difficult even to imagine a world other than the world of
civilization, which must conquer and convert the barbarian or else.
But there is another story within this story of conflict: that of the
barbarians who experience the march of civilization, if not as literal
extinction, then as an extinction of a way of life, and history as a
suppression of their voices in time. The barbarian's story is bound

up with the history of civilization: the barbarian as so defined is very much a product of civilization, without which the very notion of barbarianism becomes meaningless. Yet in their alterity, barbarians are from the moment of conception negations, castaways from history, evolutionary dead ends doomed to extinction.

The barbarian is the ultimate exile (and perhaps every exile carries a taint of the potential barbarian). The paradigmatic exile is the stranger—stranger at once to the society of origin and the society of arrival—who exists in the niches of the society of refuge. The barbarian is without even that niche, an outcast from society, the total outsider, for whom there is no refuge or acceptance, except in the total abandonment of the identity that was the cause of estrangement in the first place; in other words, by cultural extinction. There can be no partially assimilated, hyphenated barbarian. The paradigmatic barbarian is the wandering nomad.

George Simmel wrote that the stranger (read the exile: "the man who comes today and stays tomorrow") of circumstantial necessity commands an objectivity that helps unlock the hidden relations of society. The stranger as barbarian ("the wanderer who comes today and goes tomorrow") may also have much to tell us about the hidden relations of society, for in this case the estrangement is a radical estrangement from civilization itself. If we concede to the barbarian a historical presence, civilization's denial of humanity to the barbarian appears not as a confirmation of an inherent barbarity that history has demonstrated already by banishing the barbarian from its domain but as a perversion that condemns civilization itself to an alienated historical consciousness. Civilized historical consciousness is alienated in a double sense: from its own origins and from its own humanity, for the dehumanization of the barbarian dehumanizes the civilized as well.

In his *Savagism and Civilization*, Roy Harvey Pearce relates that American soldiers embarking on an expedition against the Iroquois in 1779 toasted their expedition with the words, "Civilization or death to all American savages" (51). What Pearce says of the conquest of the Indian may have something to tell us about all situations when civilization encounters the barbarian as its foe:

> Americans who were setting out to make a new society could find a place in it for the Indian only if he would become what they were—settled, steady and civilized. Yet somehow he would not be anything but what he was—roaming, unreliable, savage. So they concluded that they were destined to try and civilize him and, in trying, to destroy him, because he could not and would not be civilized. He was to be pitied for this, and also to be censured. Pity and censure were the price Americans would have to pay for destroying the Indian. Pity and censure

would be, in the long run, the price of the progress of civilization over savagism. (53)

Pearce's words resonate, with even a greater sense of tragedy, in the two novels that provide the basis for this essay: J. M. Coetzee's *Waiting for the Barbarians* and Yasar Kemal's *The Legend of the Thousand Bulls* (published in Turkey as *Bin Bogalar Efsanesi*). These two authors are vastly different in background and the literary traditions they draw upon. Coetzee is a white South African writer who consciously draws upon the European literary tradition (he has been compared, among others, to Kafka); Kemal is a Turkish writer, much more in the Third World tradition, whose writing owes much to native oral epic traditions, especially in this work. Nevertheless, what one reviewer has written of Coetzee's work could be applied equally to Kemal's writing:

> The literature of most of the world—Latin America, Eastern Europe, South Africa—is a literature of allegory and fable infused with modernist sensibility. Here, the grotesque and the fantastical are elemental, the language of hallucination is common, and the controlling metaphor is the image of a human being steadily broken by a gathering force that calls itself The State, composed of people who not only look and speak as we do but are in fact our friends, relatives, and neighbors. The urgency and sense of mission . . . is unmistakable: let the record show that at this time in this place human beings did unspeakable things to one another and suffered at each other's hands as none could have suffered through famine, flood, disease, or economic devastation. (Gornick 111)

For reasons that should become obvious below, Kemal does not use the word *barbarian* in *The Legend of the Thousand Bulls*, and much that is on the surface of Coetzee's writing—the relationship between civilization and barbarism, history and its relationship to power and to the struggle for human dignity and liberation—remains implicit rather than explicit in Kemal's work. Nevertheless, the two works share in common an indictment of civilization for the "unspeakable" deeds it justifies against the barbarian Other and are at one in the conclusion to which they point: so long as civilization denies humanity to the barbarian, it deprives itself of the claim to humanity that is its own reason for existence. In either case, it is identification with the barbarian that makes it possible to expose the negation of humanity upon which civilization nourishes itself.

Here the two works part ways. They differ radically in their narrative strategies and consequently in the critiques they offer of oppression. *Waiting for the Barbarians* is an allegory of the confrontation between civilization and barbarism that has no specific location in time or space; in it we may hear the anguish of the South African writer faced with intractable choices who, despairing of his own country's history, perhaps of all history, points to a fictional existence outside of that history as the only possibility for a humane life. The narrative voice is that of the civilized: the hero (or anti-hero) of the novel is an official of a civilization bent upon destroying the barbarians. Despairing of a civilization that manufactures barbarians, then destroys them in order to justify its own existence, he repudiates civilization and with it, history, to take refuge in the natural rhythms of barbarian existence. The barbarians appear in the novel as voiceless shadows that give the civilized occasion to reflect upon (and agonize over) the internal and highly reified contradictions of civilization.

The Legend of the Thousand Bulls, equally anguished, is nevertheless written as history, the history of the destruction of a nomadic tribe in Southern Anatolia. The destruction is inexorable and inevitable, as an expanding sedentary civilization deprives the nomads, literally, of room for existence. The civilized and the barbarians are not foreign to one another but are the very same people at different stages in the transition from barbarism to civilization. That the clash between the two ways of life appears also as a confrontation between two historical modes of production, the nomadic and the modern capitalist, endows national history with a globally allegorical significance. Kemal, like Coetzee, perceives in the negation of barbarian existence a negation of nature, but nature in this case does not provide an escape from history, since nature is also historicized as a socially constructed sensibility that at best lingers only in memory once the way of life that produced it has been extinguished. His is not just a critique of civilization, but of a particular (modern) civilization that permits no escape from history into nature, because its denial of history to the barbarian also implies the denial of a place in history to any sensibility of nature that obstructs civilization's transformative greed.

This time, moreover, the events are narrated in the voice of the barbarian, and while the barbarian faces inevitable destruction, the voice lingers in history, even displacing civilization and decentering its claims, by recalling an alternative vision of history—and nature. The struggle between civilization and barbarism appears in Coetzee's work as a struggle between history and nonhistory; Kemal brings the struggle into history, contesting civilization's claim to represent humanity with the claims of the barbarian. *The Legend of the Thousand Bulls* is not to be construed as a history or even a historical novel, but it derives much of its critical power and radical immediacy from the historicized form in which Kemal casts the narrative.

The aim of the following discussion is neither to indict civilization per se nor to privilege the barbarian but rather to raise the very inevitability of civilization's betrayal of its own premises as it barbarizes the Other and confounds civilization with power over the barbarian. The barbarian way of life is itself exclusive; it identifies humanity with membership in the immediate group. Against this, civilization can claim a broader humanity because it establishes principles of inclusion against the inclination of the barbarian to exclude the Other as "naturally" foreign.[1] It is this claim of inclusion that civilization then betrays as its principles harden into a wall across the frontier that excludes the humanity of the barbarian or, worse, serve as an excuse for the limitless expansion of its frontiers that ultimately deprives the barbarian of living space. The issue is not civilization then: it is power.

To bring this issue to the surface, it is necessary to expose the mystification that is built into the language surrounding the juxtaposition of civilization against barbarism. *Barbarism* or *barbarian* belongs in that category of terms (*savagery, primitive, anarchy* also come to mind immediately) that are irremediably mystifying; they irretrievably confound a way of life (or even a mode of production, as in Lewis H. Morgan's usage of savagery and barbarism, for example) with abstractions that are the negation of humanity. The very terminology makes it impossible to distinguish a way of life with its own historical and ecological justification, endowed with concrete forms of existence and corresponding social and natural sensibilities, from those abstract, threatening "barbarian" dispositions that, while not an exclusive property of any one human group, from the beginning come to be attached only to certain denigrated forms of social existence. The barbarian way of life is seen as forever imprisoned in barbarity. When the civilized behave in similar ways, the behavior is likewise attributed to a reversion to barbarism, covering up the possibility that what appears as a historical throwback may in fact be the very product of the logic of civilization. In the discourse of the civilized, barbarism serves the function of keeping civilization pure and clean, even when it is at its most barbaric.[2]

As with the novelists whose work I discuss, I distinguish the way of life from the characteristics attributed to it in the discourse of civilization, while retaining the term barbarian, despite all its ambiguity. The juxtaposition of the civilized against the barbarian is ideologically powerful because the terms derive their meaning from one another, rather than from any rigorous relationship to the concrete social forms that they pretend to describe. The relationship, to put it somewhat differently, is a relationship between two signifiers, with tenuous memories of the signified, let alone of an actual referent. And it is at this level that the significations must be challenged, that is, not by juggling terms but by recalling their content. To adopt different terms for describing the so-called barbarian way of life might do away with the ambiguity, but it would also bypass euphemistically the problem at hand, which is the confounding of concrete social forms with abstract human dispositions, with all the ideological implications of such confusion.

This affirmation of the barbarian way of life implies neither a romanticization of that way of life nor a nostalgia for it but instead provides an indispensable critical position on an intractable ideological problem. In the two works that I discuss, the identification with the barbarian perspective makes it possible for the authors to reveal civilization in a guise other than that of its own self-image as representative of humanity, that is, as an excuse for power, by which the powerful justify in ideology the oblivion to which in practice they consign the powerless. The barbarian voice, which the civilized believe they must suppress to achieve humanity, assumes thereby a purpose beyond that of recalling the barbarian into history; it functions as a reminder of the vulnerability of civilization to its confusion with power, which alienates civilization from its own humanity, renders it into an alienating abstraction (like barbarism) divorced from its own roots, and binds the civilized into a dehumanizing servitude at the mercy of this abstraction as inexorably as it destroys the barbarians it manufactures to rationalize its own humanity. In the subjective presence of the barbarian, the barbaric deeds civilization perpetrates are not to be excused as a throwback to a barbarian state of existence but appear for what they are: the necessary products of civilization itself, as it exists in reality rather than in the ideological imagination of the civilized.

The recovery of the barbarian way of life is not important merely for providing a critical perspective on civilization, however. There is another aspect to the problem that is equally important, if not more so: the suppression of the barbarian is also the extinction of social and ecological sensibilities at a severe cost to all humanity. The march of civilization may release new possibilities and sensibilities, but it also tramples into oblivion others, among which ecological sensibilities are paramount. The barbarian way of life, in its intimate entanglement with nature, is a fount of such sensibilities. Its suppression is like the extinction of the song in my epigraph from Chatwin, a loss of human experience in the world, a diminution of humankind's own wealth.

This point is made especially clear in *The Legend of the Thousand Bulls* and has much to do with the historical form in which Kemal casts the narrative, which traces the gradual and inexorable silencing of the barbarian's song. I suggest below that Coetzee's allegory, moving as it is as a critique of the sacrifice of civilization to power, also partakes of the very characteristics of the ideological stratagem that he criticizes because it reduces the barbarian to an abstraction that enables a self-criticism, or less charitably, a self-pity of the civilized. *Waiting for the Barbarians* wallows in that self-pity, keenly aware of the misdeeds of civilization but also utterly mystified by the barbarian, hence caught in a no-man's-land from which there is no exit. Kemal's fiction, on the other hand, is a fighting story. In casting the narrative as history, he confronts head-on the ideological suppression that is implicit in the denial of history to the barbarian. He tells a story of extinction, but the very telling of it rescues the barbarian's song from oblivion and finds in the barbarian a humanity that is every bit as concrete, legitimate, and complex as that which is found in the civilized. *The Legend of the Thousand Bulls* recalls the barbarian's voice not just in criticism but more importantly in displacement of the claims of civilization. The goal of the displacement is not to abolish civilization in a nostalgic recuperation of the barbarian way of life but to serve as a reminder that the voice of the barbarian may help liberate the civilized from their own ideological prison-house.

1. The "Empire of Pain": Civilization and Barbarism in *Waiting for the Barbarians*

The narrator (and the hero) of Coetzee's story is the magistrate of a frontier town in an empire without a specific location in time or place; it could be the central Asian steppes of a bygone day, but the names are European. The aging magistrate is a man given to the pursuit of everyday earthly pleasures, that is, eating, drinking, and womanizing. The frontier under his administration is peaceful. On the other side of the frontier are nomadic barbarians. There are other people, too, fishing folk living in the river valleys, who are even farther away in time from the sedentary civilization than the barbarians. In ordinary times, the barbarians and the townsfolk live and let live, trade, and even work with one another, their lives following the rhythms of nature, which on the frontier rule all existence. The magistrate has a hobby: excavating nearby ruins for clues to the frontier's past, possibly previous empires or the history of the barbarians themselves. But it is a hobby, not a passion, for the frontier allows him no passion. After fruitlessly spending an afternoon among the ruins, waiting for them to speak to him of the past, he mutters to himself:

Ridiculous I thought: a greybeard sitting in the dark waiting for spirits from the byways of history to speak to him before he goes home to his military stew and his comfortable bed. The space above us is merely space, no meaner or grander than the space above the shacks and tenements and temples and offices of the capital. Space is space, life is life, everywhere the same.

But as for me, sustained by the toil of others, lacking civilized voices with which to fill my leisure, I pamper my melancholy and try to find in the vacuousness of the desert a special historical poignancy. Vain, idle, misguided! How fortunate that no one sees me! (16–17)

Into this calm steps the empire in the person of Colonel Joll, an officer of the Third Bureau, a kind of special police. Colonel Joll is there to investigate rumors going around the capital that barbarians are on the move against the empire. The investigation is not in fact an investigation but rather a determined effort to prove that the barbarians are indeed on the move. Colonel Joll proceeds to take barbarian prisoners and torture them until he can get them to testify to their warlike intentions. He does not care whether his prisoners are genuine barbarians; the fishing folk are as good as the nomads, so long as he gets his "evidence." When informed of the difference, his response is: "[P]risoners are prisoners" (22).

The magistrate develops an obsession for one of these barbarians, a woman whose body has been misshapen by the colonel's torture. The obsession has all the suggestiveness of sexuality and yet it does not express itself in sex. It takes the form of a ritual washing of the barbarian woman, especially of the feet that have been broken by the colonel. Every night he washes her and slowly loses consciousness in the washing. He senses, however, that his obsession, in the absence of sex, may be nothing other than a way to get at the secrets of the barbarian, a mere variation of what her torturers have done to her, a colonization of the body that parallels the colonization of the barbarian by civilization:

[W]ith this woman it is as if there is no interior, only a surface across which I hunt back and forth seeking entry. Is this how her torturers felt hunting their secret, whatever they thought it was? . . . I behave in some ways like a lover—I undress her, I bathe her, I stroke her, I sleep beside her—but I might equally well tie her to a chair and beat her, it would be no less intimate. (43)

Sex does come in the end, but only after the magistrate finally decides to liberate the woman, to return her to her barbarian kin. But even then the magistrate is not sure of his motives: "Is it she I want," he asks himself, "or the traces of a history her body bears?" (64).

His alienation is by this time complete. As he hands the woman over to the barbarians, hoping that it will also help the empire's relations with them, he ruminates: "And here I am patching up relations between the men of the future and the men of the past, returning, with apologies, a body we have sucked dry—a go-between, a jackal of Empire in sheep's clothing!" (72).

In the meanwhile, troops have arrived in town under the command of Colonel Joll for the campaign against the barbarians. The magistrate finds himself in jail, accused of treasonous dealings with the barbarians but really, he believes, for his noncooperative attitude toward the colonel. The rest of the story is an account of the progressive dehumanization of the troops, the townspeople, and the magistrate himself under the conditions created by war. The troops drink, rape the townspeople, and steal from them. The latter, gripped by the hysteria of war, blame it all on the barbarians and readily participate in the cruelties the soldiers inflict on the barbarian stragglers brought back as prisoners. The magistrate finds his own strength to protest sapped as the physical deprivations and the mental torture he suffers reduce him to an animal state where his only concern is for physical survival. As he reflects after one bout of torture:

> I wondered how much pain a plump comfortable old man would be able to endure in the name of his eccentric notions of how the Empire should conduct itself. But my torturers were not interested in degrees of pain. They were interested only in demonstrating to me what it meant to live in a body, as a body, a body which can entertain notions of justice only as long as it is whole and well. . . . They came to my cell to show me the meaning of humanity, and in the space of an hour they showed me a great deal. (115)

Amidst all this, rumors spread that the barbarians have destroyed the armies of the empire. The hysteria of war quickly gives way to the panic of defeat. The rumors are finally confirmed when Colonel Joll arrives in town, in hasty retreat to the capital, with the few tired and hungry soldiers who have been left to him. After cleaning the town of its last few loaves of bread, the colonel leaves, his carriage stoned by the townspeople.

The frontier once again returns to its struggle for survival. The fear of barbarian revenge gradually subsides, turning into sympathy for fellow creatures facing the same problems of survival:

> In the shelter of our homes, with the windows bolted and bolsters pushed against the doors, with fine grey dust already sifting through roof and ceiling to settle on every uncovered surface, film the drinking water, grate on our teeth, we sit thinking of our fellow-creatures out in the open who at times like this have no recourse but to turn their backs to the wind and endure. (153)

The magistrate feels an obligation to write a record of what has happened, but he is not sure why, because the history he wants to set forth is a history that he repudiates:

> "No man who paid a visit to this oasis," I write, "failed to be struck by the charm of life here. We lived in the time of the seasons, of the harvests, of the migrations of the waterbirds. We lived with nothing between us and the stars. We would have made any concession, had we only known what, to go on living here. This was paradise on earth." . . . I think: "I wanted to live outside history. I wanted to live outside the history that Empire imposes on its subjects, even its lost subjects. I never wished for the barbarians that they should have the history of Empire laid upon them. How can I believe that that is cause for shame?" . . . Like much else these days, I leave it feeling stupid, like a man who lost his way long ago but presses on along a road that may lead nowhere. (154, 156)

Coetzee's is a complex vision of the relationships between civilization and barbarism, history and power, nature and history. The magistrate mourns the blooming of "the black flower of civilization" (79) not because he repudiates civilization but because civilization has betrayed itself by becoming barbaric; in the end, amid all his desire to become an "unthinking savage" (133), he emerges as a civilized person for his humaneness, for his affirmation of "lawfulness" even if it is only "second-best" to a world of real justice: "All we can do is to uphold the laws, all of us, without allowing the memory of justice to fade" (139). He condemns the Empire for breaking its own laws. On the other hand, while he reaffirms the humanity of the barbarians, he is also ambivalent about them. After defending the barbarians to an officer, he asks himself: "Do I really after all believe what I have been saying? Do I really look forward to the triumph of the barbarian way: intellectual torpor, slovenliness, tolerance of disease and death? If we were to disappear, would the barbarians spend their afternoons excavating our ruins?" (52). The same ambivalence infuses Coetzee's views of nature and history. While in the end the magistrate finds salvation from history in nature, it is because nature makes for a sense of kinship among all by the necessity it imposes for survival. The escape is also an escape from what is "natural" to all human beings: "the crime that is latent in us." On the other hand, while he repudiates history, he is also obsessed with it as a possible source of answers. Indeed, in the end it is the colonel (the empire) who radically forgets history when he queries the magistrate: "You want to go down in history as a martyr, I suspect. But who is going to put you in the history books? These border troubles are of no significance. In a while they will pass and the frontier will go to sleep for another twenty years. People are not interested in the history of the back and beyond" (114). It is the same ambivalence, however, that enables the magistrate to step outside of history to see the dialectic of civilization and barbarism in all its nakedness. We may glean Coetzee's implication from the poem "Expecting the Barbarians" by Constantine Cavafy, which, according to Peter LaSalle, served as the inspiration for the title, *Waiting for the Barbarians.*

What are we waiting for, assembled in the public square?
The barbarians are to arrive today.

Why such inaction in the Senate?
Why do the senators sit and pass no laws?

Because the barbarians are to arrive today.
What further laws can the Senators pass?
When the barbarians come, they will make the laws.

Why did our emperor wake up so early,
and sits at the principal gate of the city,
on the throne, in state, wearing his crown?

Because the barbarians are to arrive today.
And the emperor waits to receive
their chief. Indeed he has prepared
to give him a scroll. Therein he engraved
many titles and names of honor.

Why have our two consuls and the praetors come
today in their red, embroidered togas;
why do they wear amethyst-studded bracelets,
and rings with brilliant glittering emeralds;
why are they carrying costly canes today,
superbly carved with silver and gold?

Because the barbarians are to arrive today,
and such things dazzle the barbarians.

Why don't the worthy orators come as usual
to make their speeches, to have their say?

Because the barbarians are to arrive today;
and they get bored with eloquence and orations.

Why this sudden unrest and confusion?
(How solemn their faces have become.)
Why are the streets and squares clearing quickly,
and all return to their homes, so deep in thought?

Because night is here but the barbarians have not come.
Some people arrived from the frontiers,
and they said that there are no longer any barbarians.

> And now what shall become of us without any barbarians?
> Those people were a kind of solution.
>
> (18–19)

The poem ends here, and Cavafy does not say to what problem the barbarians were to provide a solution. But the poem concludes with a strong sense that without the barbarians the civilized themselves feel alone, without a clear sense of direction. An observation that Hayden White makes on the "wild man" in the European tradition may suggest an answer (the concept of wildness was closely associated with concepts of savagery and barbarism):

> The notion of "wildness" (or, in its Latinate form, "savagery") belongs to a set of culturally self-authenticating devices which includes, among many others, the ideas of "madness" and "heresy" as well. These terms are used not merely to designate a specific condition or state of being but also to confirm the value of their dialectical antitheses "civilization," "sanity," and "orthodoxy," respectively. Thus, they do not so much refer to a specific thing, place, or condition as dictate a particular attitude governing a relationship between a lived reality and some area of problematical existence that cannot be accommodated easily to conventional conceptions of the normal or familiar. (151)

Without civilization, it is impossible to conceive of the barbarian. But the reverse is also true. As White observes, civilization needs the barbarian to authenticate itself; otherwise, it has to accommodate those areas of "problematical existence" within the notion of civilization itself. In their very problematicalness, these place an enormous burden upon what it means to be civilized. Cavafy's civilized do not know what will become of them without the barbarians. The magistrate in *Waiting for the Barbarians*, having questioned civilization, does not fear death but nevertheless shrinks from "the shame of dying as stupid and befuddled as I am" (94). This brand of civilization needs the barbarians it has produced to maintain conviction in its own authenticity.

But civilization needs barbarians for another reason, as well: for the perpetuation of its power. In Coetzee's story, the values of civilization have been confounded irretrievably with the empire's power. The civilization-Empire faces a predicament in the imminent dissolving of its boundaries, which it seeks to resolve by driving a physical and emotional wedge between civilized and barbarian. In his monumental work, *The Inner-Asian Frontiers of China*, Owen Lattimore observed that the Great Wall of China was intended as much to keep the Chinese in as to keep the barbarians out. The idea of the barbarian plays a similar role at the level of metaphor, keeping the civilized together and the empire's power intact. Colonel Joll inscribes upon the backs of his barbarian prisoners the word *Enemy*, and as if by magic, the townspeople who in ordinary times are barely distinguishable from the barbarians join in the torture. The greatest crime of the magistrate, that which makes him unfit to hold office, is to confound civilized and barbarian, asserting the humanity of the latter.

As is to be expected, some reviewers have seen in Coetzee's Empire the "totalitarian state" crushing its victims (Burgess 126). This is missing the point entirely; indeed, it subverts the message of the book by restricting it to the totalitarian state, which in our day has become a code word for the barbarian. Coetzee's Empire does what it does to the barbarian not because it is totalitarian; rather, it becomes totalitarian in the process of dehumanizing the barbarian. It is the fate of the state, any state, to deny nature and the humanity of the Other, hence to lose its own. Indeed, while the magistrate displays considerable ambivalence on the question of civilization versus barbarism, he is quite straightforward in his representation of the state—any state—as a distorting intrusion upon the natural rhythms of existence:

> What has made it impossible for us to live in time, like fish in water, like birds in air, like children? It is the fault of Empire! Empire has created the time of history. Empire has located its existence not in the smooth recurrent spinning time of the cycle of the seasons but in the jagged time of rise and fall, of beginning and end, of catastrophe. Empire dooms itself to live in history and plot against history. One thought alone preoccupies the submerged mind of Empire: how not to end, how not to die, how to prolong its era. (133)

Coetzee here dissolves the distinction between civilized and barbarian, between power and its enemies. And it is ultimately power, regardless of its origins, that subverts nature and makes history. The history that he repudiates appears as the history of power, and since all history is written as the history of power, the only escape is into nature. Ultimately, the choice is not merely a choice between civilized and barbarian, but between a way of life from which abstract power is absent and one in which power inscribes itself upon nature and history. If there is an escape from this dehumanized state, it may lie in recognizing the humanity—and the history—of the barbarian:

> The people we call barbarians are nomads, they migrate between the lowlands and the uplands every year, that is their

way of life. They will never permit themselves to be bottled up in the mountains. . . . They want an end to the spread of settlements across their land. They want their land back, finally. They want to be free to move about with their flocks from pasture to pasture as they used to. . . . There is a time in the year, you know, when the nomads visit us to trade. Well: go to any stall in the market during that time and see who gets short-weighted and cheated and shouted at and bullied. See who is forced to leave his womenfolk behind in the camp for fear they will be insulted by the soldiers. See who lies drunk in the gutter, and see who kicks him where he lies. . . . Shall I tell you what I sometimes wish? I wish that these barbarians would rise up and teach us a lesson, so that we would learn to respect them. We think of the country here as ours, part of our Empire—our outpost, our settlement, our market centre. But these people, these barbarians don't think of it like that at all. We have been here more than a hundred years, we have reclaimed land from the desert and built irrigation fields and planted fields and built solid homes and put a wall around our town, but they still think of us as visitors, as transients. There are old folk among them who remember their parents telling them about this oasis as it once was: a well-shaded place by the side of the lake with plenty of grazing even in winter. That is how they still talk about it, perhaps how they still see it. . . . (50–51)

The officer to whom the magistrate speaks these lines can only respond that "these border settlements are the first line of defence of the Empire. The sooner the barbarians understand that the better" (52). And in the end all that is available to the magistrate are the words, reminiscent of Pearce's statement cited earlier, that "[w]hen some men suffer unjustly, it is the fate of those who witness their suffering to suffer the shame of it" (139). As Colonel Joll is about to crush his barbarian prisoners with a four-pound hammer, the magistrate leaps forward in his weakened state to protest: "Not with that. . . . You would not use a hammer on a beast, not on a beast. . . . 'Look!' I shout. We are the great miracle of creation! But from some blows this miraculous body cannot repair itself! . . . . Look at these men . . . MEN!" (105).

Waiting for the Barbarians provides an anguished testimonial that "at this time and in this place human beings did unspeakable things to one another." It is a powerful commentary on history, power, and civilization, and yet it leaves us without the possibility of a resolution *in* history. The novel derives its power from the ambivalence, empathy, and helpless humanism of its author who, in rejecting any easy solutions, is able to articulate the basic tragedy of the human condition; yet in divorcing the confrontation between the civilized and the barbarian from any specific history, it also suppresses the historical situation from which the novel emerged, that is, the oppression of the black population in South Africa. Abdul JanMohamed has written of it:

> Coetzee's *Waiting for the Barbarians*, a deliberate allegory, epitomizes the dehistoricizing, desocializing tendency of colonialist fiction. . . . Although the novel is obviously generated by white South Africa's racial paranoia and the guilt of its liberals, *Waiting for the Barbarians*, unlike Conrad's *Heart of Darkness*, refuses to acknowledge its historical sources or to make any allusions to the specific barbarism of the apartheid regime. The novel thus implies that we are all somehow equally guilty and that fascism is endemic to all societies. In its studied refusal to accept historical responsibility, this novel, like all "imaginary" colonial texts, attempts to mystify the imperial endeavor by representing the relation between self and other in meta-physical terms. (73)

Given the inhumanity of the situation in South Africa, it may appear self-indulgent for an author like Coetzee to set out in an allegory the intolerable condition of humanity. On the other hand, the strong indictment of state power in general that Coetzee presents is not to be overlooked. While I do not wish to suggest that this is what Coetzee has in mind, in forgoing historical specificity, the allegorical representation allows a reading that goes beyond any specific instance of oppression; without a general sense of the possibility of all states to degenerate, even anticolonial struggles may produce structures of power that reproduce the inhumanity of the states they repudiate. Had Coetzee's condemnation been restricted to the fascism of his immediate historical context, *Waiting for the Barbarians* would confirm the reading of those reviewers who see in it only a critique of totalitarianism. But by encompassing the category of the barbarian, relevant to a larger span of history and historiography, Coetzee addresses and goes beyond such a critique. Nevertheless, JanMohamed's comment on the dehistoricizing tendency of the novel is well taken. A fellow South African, Nadine Gordimer, wrote of Coetzee that he chose allegory

> out of a kind of . . . desire to hold himself clear of events and their daily, grubby, tragic consequences in which, like everybody else living in South Africa, he is up to the neck, and about which he had an inner compulsion to write. So here was allegory as a stately fastidiousness; or a state of shock. He seemed

able to deal with horror . . . only—if brilliantly—if this were to
be projected into another time and plane. (110)

The issue is not that in avoiding his immediate reality, Coetzee
leaves the reader with a guilty helplessness, that he shies away
from offering an answer to the question that he raises. The opposition that he sets up between civilization and barbarism is resolved
by an affirmation of nature against history that we can ill afford to
overlook. To quote Gordimer again (this time on another novel of
Coetzee's, *The Life and Times of Michael K*):

> The place (for survival) is the earth, not in the cosmic but in the
> plain dirt sense. The idea is the idea of gardening. And with it
> floods into the book, yet again, much more than it seemed to be
> about: the presence of the threat not only of mutual destruction
> of blacks and whites in South Africa, but of killing, every-
> where, by scorching, polluting, neglecting, charging with ra-
> dioactivity, the dirt beneath our feet. (111)

The barbarian way of life, in its closeness to nature, is a reminder
to humanity of what it has lost, of civilization's alienation from its
roots in the earth. In this sense, human survival in general becomes
contingent upon the ability of civilization to assimilate itself to the
barbarian way of life that it has repudiated. The barbarian is a key
to the recovery of humanity.

The barbarian is such a key only in a metaphorical sense, however, and this is where the problem lies. *Waiting for the Barbarians*
is highly abstract, and the people in it are "symbolic representations" (Gornick 111). What Gordimer has written of the *Life and
Times of Michael K* is equally valid of *Waiting for the Barbarians*:
"The unique and controversial aspect of this work is that while it is
implicitly and highly political, Coetzee's heroes are those who ignore
history, not make it" (110). They are also, in Coetzee's own words,
souls "untouched by doctrine, untouched by history," who can lead a
humane existence only in the interstices of history and politics, who
survive the dehumanizing power of the state by making themselves
historically and politically irrelevant (qtd. in Gordimer 111). The
barbarians are shadows without voices, an occasion for the civilized
to ruminate about what they have done to the barbarians and,
therefore, to themselves.[3] Coetzee does not repudiate the state
alone; he also repudiates politics and, with it, history. The solution
he offers—an escape from history to nature—however relevant, affords little comfort to those who are condemned to living in history.
Above all, he concedes the territory of history to the powerful. His
silent barbarians are a reminder of the humanity that needs to be
recovered, but they do not offer an alternative that may reclaim

history for a humanity at peace with nature—and, therefore, with itself—against the claims of power, because their voices are not part of a history in the making. The dialogue is between the civilized, whose everyday lives exclude the barbarian, and their conscience, which suffers the pain of exclusion. What is lost in the process is the barbarian as a living being, with all the strength and frailty that that implies.

2. "The Grief of Being Left Behind": The Barbarian Voice in History

The Legend of the Thousand Bulls, though legend, is about history, history as experienced by the barbarian. As in *Waiting for the Barbarians*, the barbarians in *The Legend of the Thousand Bulls* are nomads; but while they are as foreign as the barbarians in *Waiting for the Barbarians* to the sedentary society that is robbing them of their historical existence (perhaps even more alien, as we shall see), they are not foreigners. The story has a definite setting: Southern Turkey (in the 1950s, judging by the context). The dissolution of nomadic into sedentary life is part of the history that is told; the civilized of today is the barbarian of yesterday, the one separated from the other by no more than a generation or two. The gap that separates them is as profound as that in any encounter between civilization and barbarism, yet both are acutely aware that they are the same people. The history, therefore, is not merely the history of an encounter between the barbarian and the civilized; it is also a history of becoming foreign, as civilization divides the same people into the civilized and the barbarian, alienating the civilized from their historical roots and the barbarians from the present, the one seeking to forget the past to become civilized, the other with nothing but memories of a bygone past. The "Empire of Pain" is experienced here as "the grief of being left behind."[4] What gives the story its poignancy is the sharp awareness of the barbarians that the civilized are as much prisoners of history as they themselves and that the one has no more claim to humanity than the other. As the leader of the nomadic tribe reflects at one point on the cruelties to which they have been subjected: "They are we. We are the ones inflicting this cruelty on one another" (242).

In its structure, no less than in the issues it raises, *The Legend of the Thousand Bulls* is as "timeless" as *Waiting for the Barbarians*. Some reviewers have described the novel in its timelessness as an "epic" (Wilson 266). Yet Kemal, a very realistic writer, in a blurb attached to the Turkish edition describes it as his "most realistic novel" to date. The differences in perception are to be explained, I think, by the three kinds of time that structure the story: a cosmic time, shaped by events in the cosmos, that frames the story; a trans-historical time, the story of nomadism in history, that is heard throughout the story with the regularity of a drumbeat as the nomads contrast the glories of their past with their immediate deprivation; and a historical time, in which their experience of their immediate and inexorable extinction is chronicled. The interplay of the three kinds of time gives the immediate history its timeless, epic quality. But the story derives its reality from the immediate history being told, which in the end affirms the humanity of the barbarian. The epic magnifies the voice that the history calls to our attention. And it is in the historicity of the story that the most significant differences lies between *Waiting for the Barbarians* and *The Legend of the Thousand Bulls*.

The story is simple. The tribe searches for pasture, first in the highlands, then in the lowlands, as the seasons follow one another. The search is unsuccessful, as sedentary society denies to the tribe the land to graze their sheep, pitch their tents, or even bury their dead. In episode after episode, the tribespeople are cheated, humiliated, and abused by their sedentary brethren, as the tribe dwindles in size and gradually loses its identity. The richness of the story lies in the characters with whom Kemal peoples it, who are recognizable as social types of that particular region of Turkey, yet retain their individuality in their responses to the dilemmas with which the situation presents them. The collective story of the tribe itself is intertwined with the lives and dreams of its individual members, of whom three play an especially important part: the master craftsman Haydar, a key member of the tribe as its blacksmith, the descendant of generations of blacksmiths and the repository of tribal memory; his grandson Kerem, a little boy, who, in the midst of tribal disaster, is obsessed with his falcon; and a young woman, Ceren, who has the power to save the tribe if only she will marry out of the tribe but who refuses to, because she is in love with another member of the tribe, who has taken to the hills to escape prosecution.

The story begins on the night of May fifth of an unspecified year, which is a critical time in the tribal lore because on that night, two former mortals who have since become divine, heavenly bodies hold their annual meeting in a regeneration of nature. Anyone pure of heart who witnesses the meeting will be granted any wish uttered at the moment of the meeting. This year, the tribe is pinning on this meeting all its hopes of being granted the pasturelands that will help them survive the coming year. And yet beneath this collective wish, every member of the tribe has a private wish, from the little boy Kerem, who more than anything would like a falcon, to Ceren, who wishes to have her lover back, to the tribal elder, already a hundred years of age, who yearns for the elixir of immortality. When the meeting occurs in the early hours of the morning, it is the little boy who, half-asleep, thinks he has seen it and, in his excitement, wishes for the falcon rather than the land that the tribe needs desperately.

The little boy gets his falcon, and the tribe sets out on its hopeless search for land. The story that follows is a story of desperate tribulation and inexorable extinction. Kemal captures the intensity of the desperation in an encounter between two nomadic tribes seeking survival that pass one another one dawn in the fall:

> The two tribes faced one another on the planes in silence, not a sound to be heard from either side. . . . Like a song gone silent, they faced one another, worn-out. Each contemplated the unbelievable state of the other.
>
> Finally, the chief of the Horzum tribe rode up to the steward Suleyman:
>
> "Greetings, Suleyman," he said. His voice was hoarse. As if he was suddenly full of regret, he was unable to speak out the rest of his greeting.
>
> "Welcome, chief," said Suleyman. He moved his horse up. The two of them looked at one another, examined one another. Then at once they smiled together, bitter, tired.
>
> The chief of Horzum: "They finished us off in Cukurova," he said, barely audible. "They finished us off, Suleyman."
>
> Suleyman responded: "Finished." He could say no more, for fear that he was about to burst out in tears, like a child.
>
> The chief: "Suleyman," he said, "Our end has come. The tribes are all in the same state. They are all miserable, shattered. The nomads no longer have children, their sheep are gone. They have obliterated our roots in this cruel land. I know not what to do. I have been on horseback for ten days now. We have been unable to find even a place to camp for a night. Cukurova has become our enemy, with its dogs, its horses, its wolves, even to its birds and ants."
>
> "Enemy," Suleyman managed to mutter. And silently, imperceptibly he began to sob. The tears streamed down to his beard. The chief of Horzum, too, was about to break out in tears. He held them back, and in the effort, his whole frame shook.
>
> "What shall we do, Suleyman?"
>
> Suleyman could not answer, could not look him in the face again. He kept his gaze fixed on the neck of his horse, crying.
>
> They stood like that for a while in the mud, surrounded by the mist of the dawning day. In silence they thought back to the old days. Thoughts of the great days, of happy days, flowed through their minds in streams.
>
> The chief said, "I wish you health, Suleyman, I wish you health. . . ."

He turned his horse around and left. Suleyman could barely stay on his horse. He was unable to raise his head to look after him.

Dwindled, poor, the Horzum tribe made its way through the mud, and disappeared in silence.

In days gone, the chief of Horzum descended upon Cukurova with his thousand black tents as a flock of eagles. Cukurova could barely contain his sheep, goats and ruby-eyed horses, camels. His own tent held all in awe; with its thirty rooms, it took one week to put up and one week to take down. The blinding beauty of the carpets, the workmanship of the tent posts could not be equalled in any palace. Nobody left his tent empty-handed. Suleyman sat on his horse, struggling with himself. He tried not to think of older days, but could not resist it. In these times of death, there was a dizzying taste to thinking of the old days. He did not want to think of his past, which was embarrassing in its self-glorification. But seeing the chief of Horzum had brought back the memories in cascades.

His son had come by his side. He said to him: "Let us make camp by yonder castle, so that we can bury the child."

Duranca's child had been dead for three days, but they had not been able to stop long enough to bury the child. The mother had been carrying the corpse on her back for three days.

"Alas, the chief of Horzum, alas! I have forgotten my own misery in my grief for you. Before you Sultans and Shahs knelt in obeisance, your treasures were as the treasures of Egypt, castles fell as you burst forth from Horasan. . . . So this is your end. . . . Alas, alas, alas. . . ." (150–52)

The tribe struggles back, but with a realization that its struggle is already lost; the dead child is a symbol of the death of hope for the tribe's collective future. Even as tribe members bury their dead and, with them, their past and their future, they recognize that beyond the evils they encounter, what is constricting the life out of them is another way of life, that the sedentary "enemy" has no choice but to extinguish the nomads for its own survival. As the hopelessness of their situation becomes impossible to ignore, the same steward Suleyman "moans,"

"Why do we persist? Why do we refuse to bury this corpse that has been dead a hundred years, and now stinks to high heaven? . . . Is not what we do unspeakable? Wherever we go, we scorch the fields. How can the people of Cukurova not be our enemies? We feed to our sheep the subsistence of the poor and the helpless. Should they crown the thieves of their crops?" (241)

In this desperation, two hopes remain to the tribe. One is for Ceren to marry the son of a local landlord, who is hopelessly in love with her and follows the tribe around in its tribulations. This might provide them with land on the landlord's holdings. But Ceren refuses, remaining loyal to her beloved, though rumor has it that he is already dead. Although her refusal slowly turns the tribe against her, the steward is unwilling to force her into a marriage she does not want. So they turn to their second hope, even though they are convinced of its futility: a sword that the blacksmith has been at work on for the past thirty years. In older times, swords of that quality brought to nomads the reverence and munificence of emperors. Now, they hope, it might bring them a piece of land. So Haydar sets out with his sword, the past ringing in his ears, to search out in the city former nomads, kin to the tribe who have become local notables and may help the tribespeople in their plight. Those who are in a position to help give the old craftsman little beyond their pity, while the ones who admire his sword are in no position to help. In his desperation he ends up in the capital, Ankara, convinced that Ismet Pasha, hero of the revolutionary war, will recognize the sword for what it is. When he manages to catch a glimpse of Ismet, the latter hurries away in embarrassment as his assistants coax the old nomad away.

Haydar returns to the tribe. His last act before he dies is to melt the sword and forge a mysterious symbol, whose shape the tribespeople recognize as an ornament on their carpets but nothing more. Their hopes now turn to Ceren, who has finally consented to marry the landlord's son. Before the marriage can take place, however, her beloved returns, she turns back to him, and the last hope of the tribe is gone.

A year elapses. It is once again the fifth of May, and the occasion for wishing presents another chance to the tribe, which is now half the size it had been the year before. But the tribe is no longer a tribe in spirit. The collective goal is gone. The last event in the book is the murder of Ceren's lover, the descendant of tribal chiefs, by the tribespeople. At that point, Kemal refers the end of the tribe to the same natural cycle that began it:

> It is the same every year. On the night that connects the fifth to the sixth of May, the two divines Hizir and Ilyas meet some place in the world. At the moment of their meeting, all life stops, all the living die. Immediately thereafter they are reborn, more alive, more prolific. The two stars, one from the west, the other from the east, meet in the middle of the heavens, touch one another and unite. They form a ball of light, and scatter all over the world. (347)

These last lines contain not just a negation but also an affirmation of the possibility that out of the dying will come a new life. The story that *The Legend of the Thousand Bulls* tells is that of an inevitable end, but epics or—as the author prefers, legends—do not die. They remain in historical memory long after the people who lived them are gone, decentering the history that has replaced theirs and regenerating it by recalling the humanity that has been extinguished. As the novel ends with the tribe's death, Kemal recalls the history of the nomads, here told as epic, the lines of which appear throughout the story as the counterpoint to the immediate story of death:

> We migrated out of Horasan. . . . Like herds of wolves, we spread all over the world, from east to west. We rode our ruby-eyed, long-necked horses to the Indus, to the Nile. We conquered countries, castles, cities; we established states. . . . On the plains of Haran, thousands of us blended with the deer in whirling dances, like the great falcon. We held great feasts, we added to the great multitudes. We rode from sea to great sea in waves, moved from shore to shore. Castles, cities, countries, races, noble families bent before us. We made a whole era our captive. We did the unspeakable to many a human being. But we never looked down on them. . . . We gave our names to rivers, plains and mountains. In Anatolia, we stamped every inch of land with our presence, gave it our names; so that our lines would not be forgotten here and there, rotting in the soil. Our roots were like a rich spring, great and endless, but we spread, scattered and dwindled, exhausted and finished. Now no one will sing our songs or dance our dances. The moon will not rise or set as we see it. No one will know our laws, our traditions, our experiences, or what we see in the budding tree, hear in the blowing wind, or think of life or death. Nobody will know of the strength that comes of our feeling of being one with every living creature. . . . (324–26)

The same affirmation is there in the mysterious symbol that the blacksmith forges just before his death. Even the tribe no longer remembers what the symbol means, but the symbol remains. The melting of the sword may mean the end of an era in the history of the nomad, but the nomads will live in historical memory, if only as a symbol.

The Legend of the Thousand Bulls parallels *Waiting for the Barbarians* in the antagonistic relationship it sets up between civilization and nature. The extinction of the nomads is the extinction not only of the barbarian but also of a way of life and of a certain relationship to nature. It may not be coincidental that in their critique of civilization, both authors focus on the nomad, whose very existence is bound up with the rhythms of nature, and who, therefore, comes to represent nature itself. It is also ironic that for all the nomads' peripatetic existence, this relationship with nature gives the nomad a better appreciation of the sanctity of land than is the case for the civilized, even for the sedentary farmers of Kemal's story. The tractors that "devour the land, and howl like monsters as they do so" (9) appear with regularity in the background of the story. "We are dead. We are struggling for our last breath," the blacksmith says in the midst of his travels to the cities, and continues:

> But they too will live only until their land has rotted away. Their land is rotten, very rotten. . . . We wore out our land in a thousand years, they have rotted theirs in twenty. That much is clear. They devour their land very quickly. Or else their roots never reached the depths of the soil, and will never reach them. Like a hurricane, they move the world upside down. . . . Their lands are already rotten. (271)

In the case of *The Legend of the Thousand Bulls*, however, the civilization in question is not just any civilization, but modern civilization. The immediate story the novel tells is the last phase of a history that began in 1876 when a great nomad rebellion in Southern Turkey was suppressed by the Ottoman government, and the nomads were presented with the choice of settling down to a sedentary life they did not wish—or extinction. The conflict was part of the struggle of the Ottoman state to make itself into a modern state. Those nomads who somehow escaped the suppression and continued their nomadic existence have become, even in their marginality, an embarrassment to the state and an obstacle to its efforts to modernize. As a local official tells the nomads: "For years now we have had to deal with you people. We have to put aside everything, we have to put aside development, and waste our energies on you people" (254).

But the state represents only the political face of a process that reaches deeper in society. Unlike the barbarians in *Waiting for the Barbarians*, who can escape from civilization into a natural existence, this civilization in its dynamism and expansionism allows for no living space outside itself. While Kemal at no point in the story refers to capitalism, the civilization in question is the civilization of modern capitalism. The land that to the nomads is sacred has lost its sanctity because it has become a commodity, valuable not in itself but merely as a further means to produce wealth. The question Kemal raises is a question of different languages, based on different systems of exchange and value. This is underlined in the blacksmith's futile efforts to exchange his sword for land, the sword that is the product not only of thirty years of effort but perhaps, even more importantly, of a tradition of craftsmanship that goes back to the origins of time. In older times, swords that were not nearly the equal to his in workmanship and effort inspired awe in the beholder and brought to nomads honor and gifts. He finds to his great surprise that his sword invokes nothing more than a begrudging admiration and bemusement at the foolishness of an old craftsman who believes that he can exchange it for land, which is a means for the production of exchange-value within capitalism, as the sword is not. The shock that kills him in the end is the shock of his realization that he does not wish to be part of a world that no longer speaks his language. The melting of the sword to forge the long-forgotten symbol of his craft is his last act of defiance against that world.

Within a specifically Turkish context, this repudiation of the nomad in a new language of modernity carries its own meaning. It is not simply the marginalization of the barbarian by civilization or a rejection of the past in the name of the present: it is also a repudiation by a people of their own roots. For in their own historical consciousness, in the very mythology of Turkish nationalism, Turks are the descendants of nomads. The extinction of nomadism in practice contrasts dramatically with the glorification of a nomadic past at the level of ideology.[5] In articulating this contradiction between national self-image and national history, between ideology and practice, the story that Kemal tells, in its very historicity, challenges the claims of the ideology and decenters the national history written around that ideology.

In contrast to *Waiting for the Barbarians*, therefore, the confrontation between civilization and barbarism, between civilization and nature, is not dissolved here into a choice between history and nature but appears rather as an irresolvable contradiction between two histories: the history of a modern nation that recalls its nomadic past as an emblem of national identity within a language of modernity that dissolves all identity into the universal language of commodity exchange; and history as recalled by the nomads themselves, which reveals this modern history to be ideological, sustaining its claims as national history only by suppressing its own past.

There is nothing in this alternative history to feed national parochialism or chauvinism. Kemal's portrayal of the nomad is anything but romantic, for the world of the nomad that emerges from *The Legend of the Thousand Bulls* is as cruel in the end as the world that extinguishes nomadic existence. They are human not because they are more humane than others, but because they are as vulnerable as anyone else. What makes them worth recalling is not the glory they might bring to a national past but a way of life that has something to say about the fetishism of modernity that shapes the Turkish present. It is in this critique of modernity that the barbarian voice forces upon our consciousness, articulating an antimodernist reading of the national past.

However, Kemal's work is not merely a negative operation of displacing the claims of a modern Turkish civilization. The recalling of the barbarian voice is intended not as an epitaph to the barbarian or even as a condemnation of the civilization that has destroyed the barbarian. The barbarian voice is instead a reminder of what civilization loses in destroying the barbarian. The ultimate goal is to recover what may help restore to civilization some sense of its own predicament and redirect its course in history. When the author writes that "the moon will not rise or set as we see it," he speaks of an experience that has been lost to humanity as a whole. This is the case even with the less desirable aspects of the nomads' behavior which, however ruthless their consequences ("we did the unspeakable to many a human being"), nevertheless had their counterpoint in nomadic mores rooted in ethical values that are the common legacy of humankind. The argument here is similar to the one that Michel de Certeau offers in his "Montaigne's 'Of Cannibals': The Savage 'I,'" in which he says of Montaigne's essay that it "is inscribed within . . . [a] heterological tradition in which the discourse about the other is a means of constructing a discourse authorized by the other," in which the barbarian voice serves as an occasion for reflecting upon the civilized (68). Recognition of an ethical basis to the behavior of the barbarian is a key element: "Cannibalism, because it is approached from the angle of the victim (the heroism of the vanquished) and not the perpetrator, brings to light an ethic of faithfulness in war; and polygamy, because it is seen from the point of view of service (the 'solicitude' of the women), not masculine domination, similarly reveals a superior degree of conjugal fidelity" (de Certeau 75). The values, of course, are the values that the civilized share, which at once renders problematic the condemnation of the cannibals for their cannibalism or polygamy, but which also reflects back upon what the civilized do in the name of "faithfulness in war" or "conjugal fidelity." Kemal's discourse follows a similar procedure. By reaching out for the ethical bases of the nomads' behavior, he brings them close to the experience and concerns of the civilized and underlines the shared values of the civilized and the barbarian. Thus, Kerem's love for the falcon is rooted in a boy's dream of freedom; Ceren's loyalty to the memory of her supposedly dead lover affirms the importance of fidelity; the tribe's unwillingness to force her into a marriage she does not want reveals respect for this fidelity and respect for women; the hidden personal dream whose fulfillment each member wishes of the divines even points to the presence of the unexpected—a concern for the individual over the community. The list need not be prolonged. Presented in the voice of the nomad, nomadic experience ceases to be foreign or barbaric and confirms a universal discourse on humanity.

Writing of early European accounts of the Americas, Tzvetan Todorov observes that those writers who sought to incorporate the voice of the Indians into their accounts (in other words, the history of the conquest as seen by the Indians) initiated a "dialogue of cultures" with significant consequences: "a dialogue in which no one has the last word, in which neither voice is reduced to the status of a simple object, and in which we gain advantage from our external-ity to the other" (250). The consequences, after three centuries of colonization that have brought in their wake the incorporation of the voices of the colonized into a global discourse, are that

> The representatives of Western civilization no longer believe so naively in its superiority, and the movement of assimilation is running down in that quarter, even if the recent or ancient nations of the Third World still want to live like the Europeans. On the ideological level, at least, we are trying to combine what we regard as the better parts of both terms of the alternative; we want *equality* without compelling us to accept identity; but also *difference* without its degenerating into superiority/inferi-ority. (Todorov 249)

What Todorov speaks of is not cultural relativism but cultural pluralism. The globally democratic implications of such cultural plu-ralism are evident; so are the antidemocratic consequences of a cul-tural parochialism that suppresses the voices of alternative ways of life. Ironically, the people who learned democracy from Europe may have something of their own to contribute to contemporary consid-erations of democracy, which in turn may be crucial to global sur-vival. Writing of recent Indian declarations in the Americas, de Cer-teau notes that these declarations, in addition to their plea for cultural pluralism, introduce two revolutionary ideas into a global discourse: reorganization of polities into a federation of self-man-aging communities, in a way that reintroduces into political think-ing the notion of a collective social contract that militates against increasing subjection to centralized compulsion; and a sensibility of "collective contracts with the earth," which restores "nature" into history against a western development that, "because of the favor accorded industrialization and social conflict, has created a 'history' for itself in which 'nature' only figures as an *object* of labor and the *terrain* of socioeconomic struggles" (de Certeau 230).

This ultimately is the meaning, I think, of reintegrating into his-tory the voice of the barbarians destroyed by history. The voice will not bring back the barbarians themselves, for "there are no longer any barbarians," nor is it a plea for a return to barbarism. Rather, against a history of the inexorable march of civilization, it is a reminder that the same march appears from alternative perspectives as the suppression of the barbarians and their voices, ultimately a suppression of the very humanity of civilization, which, as Kemal has it, leaves its bits and pieces "here and there, rotting in the soil." It is a reminder to the civilized, in other words, of the necessity of recapturing their own exhausted humanity and, with it, their own say over history.

3. Conclusion: History and the Critique of Civilization

Waiting for the Barbarians and *The Legend of the Thousand Bulls* both offer profound critiques of civilization as power, critiques made possible by recalling the barbarian into history. The two works differ sharply, however, in the perspective they adopt toward history. *Waiting for the Barbarians* so thoroughly equates history with the history of power that it leaves escape from history into an ahistorical nature as the only response to oppression. *The Legend of the Thousand Bulls* brings the story of the barbarian, as told by the barbarian, into history, which necessitates the rewriting of history because it introduces the barbarian voice into history as a subject—thereby problematizing the relationship between nature and history. This establishes unequivocally that any solution to oppression must be found within history, that is to say, the social relations that constitute history. At the very least, it serves to decenter an abstract notion of civilization as the sole datum of history.

The political implications of these two perspectives on history are transparent. Coetzee's fiction presents the oppression of the barbarian by the civilized as a permanent feature of the human condition and thereby appears to reject political solutions to the problem of oppression. His barbarians are for the most part silent shadows who lead an existence outside the confines of civilization. As Gordimer notes, his novels contain no suggestion of the real-life struggle of the barbarian against the civilized (in this case, the black against the white population of South Africa) that is raging around him (111). It may not be fair to charge him with complicity in the inhuman oppression of the black population of South Africa, as JanMohamed suggests, but the rejection of politics in his writing may explain why, in spite of his profound critique of power, he is able to survive as a writer under an oppressive regime.

Kemal, on the other hand, has been accused of being a Marxist by the Turkish regime, and if he has avoided punishment for his writings, it may be that it is his international reputation as a writer that has saved him. There is little in his writings that could be construed as Marxist in any strict political sense, of course; rather, what renders his writing politically dangerous is his questioning of the ideological and political assumptions of the regime, a questioning that derives its force from the immediacy of the social reality that he depicts. His rewriting of history in the voice of the barbarian displaces the self-image of the civilization upon which political power rests and calls into question the very assumptions that justify the authority of a regime that perceives itself as the civilizing, because modernizing, force in society. His barbarians are not merely objects of "pity and censure," to recall Pearce's words, but counter the claims to civilization of the society that destroys them by asserting their own humanity against it.

I would like to conclude here with an example intended to show that the questions raised by these works are not merely questions of remote and troubled Third World societies, but are issues that continue to perplex our quest for a humane and civilized existence. In his essay on wildness, Hayden White suggests that the extension of knowledge has "demythologized" concepts such as wildness and barbarism (153). While we may no longer attribute beastly disfigurations to the barbarian as was the case with premodern portrayals,[6] the notion of the barbarian as a threat to civilization is very much alive, even as that civilization becomes ever more global and transnational. The persistence of this notion helps perpetuate oppression, not only of the barbarian but of the civilized, as well, justifying it by appeal to the threat of barbarism and alienating contemporary civilization from its own aspirations. History plays a major part in this continued distancing of people from one another.

In its 30 November 1987 issue, *Time* magazine published a report on Gaza under the heading "A Land That History Forgot." Two weeks later Gaza erupted into history in an insurrection that has left an indelible impression on our consciousness and perhaps even changed the historical course of the relationship between Israel and its Palestinian subjects. History might have forgotten Gaza, but obviously History did not include everyone. The content of the *Time* report contradicted its title. The report was accompanied by a photograph of two Palestinian women walking by, as the caption told the reader, "under the watchful eyes of an Israeli solder," armed with an assault rifle. Neither the Israeli soldier nor those who had sent him there had forgotten Gaza. Nor had the Palestinian people to whom the soldier and the gun were continuous reminders of their historical situation. When they rose in insurrection two weeks later, the insurrection did not bring them back into history—for we may safely suppose that they thought they were in history all along—but rather asserted their historical consciousness against a History that sought to forget them.

What renders the *Time* report on the Gaza significant is the endowment of *History* in its title with anthropomorphic subjectivity, the forgetting of Gaza not by *Time* magazine, or those for whom it speaks, but by History. The usage immediately calls to mind Karl Marx's statement in the *Holy Family* that

> *History* does *nothing*; it "does *not* possess immense riches," it "does *not* fight battles." It is *men*, real, living men, who do all this, who possess things and fight battles. It is not "history" which uses men as a means of achieving—as if it were an individual person—*its* own ends. History is *nothing* but the activity of men in pursuit of their ends. (63)

History does not forget either, we may add; men and women do. But the forgetting is easier, indeed appears as the work of History, when the objects of forgetting are barbarians. Furthermore, barbarians are the extreme case that illustrates what happens to others similarly situated within power, states, nations, and economies: those whom societies suppress by forgetting or oppress by silencing (diasporas, minorities in ghettos, the Others of the nation-state) are situated along a continuum within civilization, as the barbarian is beyond its borders.

As Marx understood very well, the distancing of history from its living subjects, which is implicit in its reification, conceals a power relationship. Conversely, I may suggest on the basis of this discussion that the reintroduction into history of the barbarian voice inevitably culminates in the critique of power. The ideologists of power, of whom we may cite Allen Bloom in his *The Closing of the American Mind* as a prominent example, are keenly aware of this and resist therefore the introduction of the voice of the Other into our understanding of the World.[7] We may argue here that what is at issue is more than transient political power. What is at issue is our ability to take responsibility for history, to establish human control over the future of humanity. The reification of history ultimately results in a fetishization of history, the relinquishing to an abstraction of a subjective power to determine the future; in other words, the process alienates from us a history that is the product of human activity. This may authorize our version of civilization by identifying it with history, but the same oblivion it therefore projects upon the barbarian also incarcerates the civilized in the prison-house of an abstraction of their own making. Restoration of the barbarian's voice to history, introducing into our consideration of the future the pluralistic possibilities made available by the suppressed voices of the past and the present, may likewise help liberate the humanity of the civilized themselves.

Notes

I would like to acknowledge my debt to Ken Berger of the Reference Department, the Perkins Library of Duke University, for his kind assistance in locating the reviews of these two books. I am also indebted for their stimulating comments to Ted Fowler, Marty Miller, and Masao Miyoshi, and to the participants in the discussion at the Harvey Goldberg Center for the Study of Contemporary History, University of Wisconsin–Madison, where this paper was first presented—especially my friend and colleague Mauri Meisner, who arranged the visit. All translations from Kemal are by me.

1. There are many examples of the identification of tribal members with the word *man* in anthropological literature. For a touching example of one barbarian who, having lost all his tribe, learns to extend the word *man* to those outside of his tribe, see Kroeber.

2. For a recent discussion of this point, see Bauman. Walter Benjamin captured the same idea concisely when he wrote that "there is no document of civilization which is not at the same time a document of barbarism" (Benjamin 258).

3. It is noteworthy that in two of Coetzee's novels, the barbarian figure suffers from voicelessness: from speech defects (*The Life and Times of Michael K.*) or complete silence because of dumbness (*Foe*). To the extent that barbarians assimilate civilization and gain speech (*The Narrative of Jacobus Coetzee*), on the other hand, they appear as degenerates who have broken with the virtues of barbarism only to become caricatures of civilization. Interestingly, Coetzee himself points to the silence of the black characters as a general characteristic of South African literature, imposed upon it by its circumstances. Referring to pastoral writing in South Africa, he observes: "Pastoral in South Africa therefore has a double tribute to pay. To satisfy the critics of rural retreat, it must portray labour; to satisfy the critics of colonialism, it must portray white labour. What inevitably follows is the occlusion of black labour from the scene: the black man becomes a shadowy presence flitting across the stage now and then to hold a horse or serve a meal. In more ways than one the logic of the pastoral mode itself thus makes the incorporation of the black man—that is, of the black serf, man, woman, or child—into the larger picture embarrassing and difficult. For how can the farm become the pastoral retreat of the black man when it *was* his pastoral home only a generation or two ago? . . . The constraints of the genre therefore make silence about the black man the easiest of an uneasy set of options" (*While Writing* 5). I might note here that an anonymous reader of this article disagreed vehemently with my reading of Coetzee and *Waiting for the Barbarians*, especially with my equation of the magistrate with Coetzee. According to this reader, my reading (as well as those of critics such as JanMohamed) is "consistently blind to the fact that in *Waiting*, Coetzee stages a thoroughgoing and relentless interrogation—an immanent critique, if you like—of the discourse of white South African liberalism in the years of what Nadine Gordimer has called 'the interregnum'—i.e., after 'Soweto' (1976), and before the collapse of apartheid." I readily concede that this is a possibility, and the essays in *White Writing*, not to speak of the passage I have just quoted, would seem to confirm criticism of my reading. In an alternate reading, the magistrate in the novel, rather than being Coetzee's own alter ego, might be representative of the "white writers" of whom Coetzee speaks. While I am not a specialist on Coetzee or South African writing, however, I fail to see on the basis of Coetzee's fiction (in contrast with his critical writings) how and where he provides an alternative to the "white writing" that he criticizes. This, and the concession of the reader that it is possible to read Coetzee as I have read him, has led me to decide in favor of retaining the original reading. My concern in this essay, at any rate, is not ultimately with Coetzee but rather with the contrasting implications of historical versus ahistorical representations of the barbarian. I hope the discussion above has made it clear, moreover, that while my reading of *Waiting for the Barbarians* may be similar to that of critics such as JanMohamed, I am much less ready than they are to dismiss an allegorical representation of the problem. If Coetzee is not given to "agony," as my anonymous reader suggests, his analysis of "white writing" nevertheless is revealing of wide-spread agonizing among white writers. I also find somewhat disingenuous, I might add, Coetzee's representation of a central ideological problem as a matter of "constraints of the genre."

4. This is from the lines of a poem by a Turkish poet, Melih Cevdet Anday, with which Kemal prefaces his tale:

> Nightly the braves mourn in the graveyard
> Weary of confounding the stars for flocks of sheep
> (They) think back to the old days . . . before the settlement
> The grief of being left behind is potent indeed.

5. For a critical discussion of the place of the nomad in contemporary Turkish historical consciousness and education, see Avcioglu.

6. Even this may need qualification. In his recently published study of the mutual images propagated by Americans and Japanese during World War II, John Dower relates that American propaganda consistently represented the Japanese as monkeys. One example he gives is especially pertinent here: the picture of a gorilla with the gun of "civilization" pointed at its head. See Dower 86.

7. Bloom's *The Closing of the American Mind* is an ideological (and deceptive) work, which, while it purports to show the way to reopening minds that have been closed since the radical 1960s, may indeed be read as a plea for closing out of American education the new and more complex understanding of the world made possible by social history, feminist scholarship, and awareness of race and the Third World in general. It is clear at any rate that Bloom would rather converse with the ancients than with his contemporary neighbors. While that is his privilege, casting doubt on the integrity of those who would rather do otherwise is not. According to Bloom, there are some among those who study other societies who are honest scholars because they "love" the "cultures" they study but the majority are merely "demagogues." Since Bloom has a clear idea of where Civilization is to be found and wears his parochialism as a badge of honor, we must assume that listening to the voice of the Other and the whole argument for cultural pluralism (which should not be confounded with cultural relativism, as he does) must appear to him as the utmost in demagoguery. His misanthropic and misandrogynous view of the world, however, is merely the expression in academic guise of the fears of a power elite that hears in the voices of the other not the promise of a more democratic and humane world but a threat to its own hegemony. Its most recent target is so-called political correctness, which is but a reductionist vulgarization of efforts to open up academic curricula to different voices. Led by no less a figure than the president of the United States, this elite seeks to cover up its ideological anxieties by misrepresenting the democratization of education as its restriction and portraying as a negation of western civilization efforts to understand it from alternative perspectives, within the context of other civilizations.

Works Cited

Avcioglu, Dogan. *Türklerin Tarihi* [*The History of the Turks*]. Vol. 1. Istanbul: Tekin Yayinevi, 1978. 2 vols.

Bauman, Zygmunt. *Modernity and the Holocaust*. Ithaca, New York: Cornell UP, 1989.

Benjamin, Walter. "Theses on the Philosophy of History." *Illuminations*. Ed. Hannah Arendt. New York: Harcourt, 1968.

Bloom, Allen. *The Closing of the American Mind*. New York: Simon and Schuster, 1988.

Burgess, Anthony. "The Beast Within: *Waiting for the Barbarians*." Rev. of *Waiting for the Barbarians*, by J. M. Coetzee. *New York Magazine* 26 April 1982. Rpt.in *Contemporary Literary Criticism* 23 (1983): 126.

Cavafy, Constantine. *The Complete Poems of Cavafy*. Trans. Rae Dalven. New York: Harcourt, 1961.

Certeau, Michel de. "Montaigne's 'Of Cannibals': The Savage 'I.'" *Heterologies: Discourse on the Other*. Minneapolis: U of Minnesota P, 1986. Vol. 17 of *Theory and History of Literature*. 67–79.

———. "The Politics of Silence: The Long March of the Indians." *Heterologies: Discourse on the Other*. Minneapolis: U of Minnesota P, 1986. Vol 17 of *Theory and History of Literature*. 225–33.

Coetzee, J. M. *Waiting for the Barbarians*. New York: Penguin, 1980.

———. *White Writing: On the Culture of Letters in South Africa*. New Haven: Yale UP, 1988.

Dower, John W. *War Without Mercy: Race and Power in the Pacific War*. New York: Pantheon, 1986.

Gordimer, Nadine. "The Idea of Gardening." Rev. of *Life and Times of Michael K*, by J. M. Coetzee. *New York Review of Books* 2 Feb. 1984. Rpt. in *Contemporary Literary Criticism* 33: 109–11.

Gornick, Vivian. "When Silence Speaks Louder than Words." Rev. of *Waiting for the Barbarians*, by J. M. Coetzee. *The Village Voice* 20 March 1984. Rpt. in *Contemporary Literary Criticism* 33 (1985): 111–12.

JanMohamed, Abdul. "The Economy of Manichean Allegory: The Function of Racial Difference in Colonialist Literature." *Critical Inquiry* 12 (Autumn 1985): 73.

Kemal, Yasar. *The Legend of the Thousand Bulls [Bin Bogalar Efsanesi]*. Istanbul: Cem Yayinevi, 1981.

Kroeber, Theodora L. *Ishi in Two Worlds: A Biography of the Last Wild Indian in North America*. Berkeley: U of California P, 1961.

Lattimore, Owen. *Inner Asian Frontiers of China*. Boston: Beacon, 1962.

Marx, Karl. *The Holy Family*. *Karl Marx: Selected Writings in Sociology and Social Philosophy*. Ed. T. B. Bottomore. New York: McGraw-Hill, 1956.

Morgan, Lewis Henry. *Ancient Society*. New York: Henry Holt, 1907.

Pearce, Roy Harvey. *Savagism and Civilization: A Study of the Indian and the American Mind*. Berkeley: U of California P, 1988.

Simmel, George. "The Stranger." *On Individuality and Social Forms*. By Simmel. Ed. Donald N. Levine. Chicago: U of Chicago P, 1971. 143–49.

Todorov, Tzvetzan. *The Conquest of America*. Trans. Richard Howard. New York: Harper, 1984.

White, Hayden. "The Forms of Wildness: Archaeology of an Idea." *Tropics of Discourse: Essays in Cultural Criticism*. Baltimore: The Johns Hopkins UP, 1986. 150–82.

Wilson, David. Rev. of *Waiting for the Barbarians*, by J. M. Coetzee. *Times Literary Supplement* 12 Nov. 1976. Rpt. in *Contemporary Literary Criticism* 29 (1984): 266.

Diaspora 1:3 1991

A Host Country of Immigrants That Does Not Know Itself

Dominique Schnapper
Ecole des Hautes Etudes en Sciences Sociales,
Paris, France
Translated by Lorne Shirinian

France's relationship with immigrants cannot be understood unless two essential aspects of its history are drawn together: the low birthrate of the French population over the past two centuries and the traditions of a nation-state propelled by a universalizing political project. The conjuncture of these two characteristics constitutes the character of the French stance toward immigrants.

1. French Specificity

As far as demography is concerned, France is unique in Europe: the decline of the birthrate began there a century earlier than in other countries. One finds Germans, Scandinavians, Italians, and Spaniards in North and South America, Australia, and New Zealand but nearly no French, because, while most European countries were exporting population at least until the Second World War, France was importing them. Its low birthrate forced it to recruit engineers, workers, and soldiers from beyond its borders. Since the middle of the nineteenth century, economic development and national defense have both depended on the entry of English, German, Belgian, Swiss, Italian, Spanish, Portuguese, and North African citizens, to cite only the most numerous waves, and on the transformation of their children into French citizens.

This demographic weakness raised an especially acute problem, since France distinguished itself, from the political point of view, by a national project of universal dimensions and by a nation-state tradition that assumed political unity would, or could, be made to coincide with cultural unity. In effect, since 1789 France has thought of itself as a political and moral example, as the country of the great Revolution and the apostle of the rights of man, as an imperial power entrusted with a mission to spread civilization to the rest of the world. Moreover, it is paradoxical that France was building a colonial empire, while its own population was increasing only as a result of immigration.

France, the nation-state par excellence, inheritor of the political and cultural centralization implemented by the monarchy in the person of the king and reinforced by revolutionary legitimacy and the Jacobin tradition, required that political and cultural unity be reinforced and manifested by the use of a common language and by reference to a common history. Any cultural particularism, be it Breton, Jewish, or Italian, appeared to be a menace to national unity. The Third Republic, imposing the same program in all the schools of all the provinces of France, excluding any regional or national particularisms, was charged with and succeeded in transforming little Bretons, Corsicans, and Provençals, the sons of miners—Italian and Polish peasants—and the children of the Jewish proletariat of Central Europe into citizens of the French Republic, speaking the same language and sharing the same cultural references, despite the violent, xenophobic feelings and explosions that continually accompanied the process.

This policy was obviously born of economic need: the iron and steel works of Lorraine were based upon the labor of Italian immigrants, just as the coal mines of the North depended upon the labor of miners systematically recruited in Poland during the 1920s. This policy was also linked to the needs of the army, as the preamble of the law of 1889 on nationality reminds us. But it was transfigured by patriotism, by the image of France as a country of liberty and the rights of man. French people doubted neither the superiority of their genius and happiness, nor the fact that those who were going to become French and participate in a glorious national destiny would recognize the same. Among the immigrants, some shared this belief (see Green).

This combination of low birthrate, national ambition, and the blurring of differences between political and cultural unity explains, among other things, the fact that France has been, until very recently, a host country for immigrants without recognizing itself as such. If the French state had neither an immigration policy nor an organization to manage such a policy, this is because the state denied the existence of immigration. The course followed with regard to immigrant children established on French soil was not to take into account their foreign origin but rather to socialize them in school, church, the army, and work, like native-born children and adolescents. It is through these national institutions, which addressed the entire population with the same methods, that the socialization of the children of immigrants came about, not through compensating and particularist institutions, whose very existence was contradictory to national ideology. The example of the Poles in the 1930s, who organized their own schools and their own Catholic missions, published newspapers in their own language, and maintained national associations, was unique. The Italian missions were never able to unify their émigrés in the same manner.

Nationality legislation was aimed at privileging and even imposing this Gallicization of the children of immigrants in France. If, of all the European countries, France is the one whose legislation gives greatest consideration to *droit du sol,* that is because France is the only European nation whose population was constituted to such an extent by immigration. The law of 1851, which gave from birth the title of French citizen to any individual born in France of parents of foreign descent also born there (commonly called dual droit du sol, or *juris soli* in international law), was intended to make these children subject to military duty. (This law also granted young people the option of giving up their right to French citizenship upon reaching majority; this option was frequently chosen as a way of evading military service.) Later, the law of 1889 actually denied such children any possibility of giving up their citizenship and military duty. For children born in France of parents born abroad, the law of 1889 provided three ways of becoming French citizens. Such children could declare themselves French, could enlist or accept recruitment, or could reside in France at the age of 21. The alternative was to refuse French nationality explicitly in the year following majority. Legislators thus organized a mechanism that made the refusal of French nationality more difficult for children born in France to immigrants. They counted on negligence in order to subject such youth to the obligations of military service. The Senate reporter did not hide it: "The individual thus declared French, finding himself on the census rolls, will be obliged, if he wishes to escape military service, to refuse the title of French citizen in the year that follows his majority and to prove that he has retained his parents' nationality. As this proof will be rarely furnished, a deplorable abuse in the greatest number of cases will be eliminated" (Long 25). Through these examples, we see that the right of nationality has had the function of accelerating the process of Gallicization, which was almost forced upon the children of people of foreign origin settled on French soil.

2. The French Lack of Knowledge

France's refusal to think of itself as a host country for immigrants explains its ignorance of ways of integrating foreign populations: the French study badly a phenomenon whose very existence is masked by national ideology. If today there is a consciousness of this phenomenon, it is because it is no longer taken for granted and because France is questioning its own identity. Until recently, neither sociologists nor historians have been inclined to explore the ways in which new French citizens behaved within the French nation. Historians of education have not sought to understand the behavior in school of young foreigners destined to become French citizens upon reaching their majority, although recent evidence recalls the sometimes xenophobic and brutal attitude of certain teachers in the Belle Epoque. Army historians teach us nothing about the participation of young recruits of foreign origin. We know only that during World War I, they paid the same tribute to war and sacrificed their lives with the same heroism as the rest of the French Army. The only protests that happened were those of politically committed groups, not new French citizens. The melting pot had functioned, perhaps in a painful manner, accompanied by violence and its xenophobic crises, but it had been efficient.

In the 1930s, the work of sociologists did incline toward foreigners (but not French citizens of foreign origin), as in Mauco's book, *Les Etrangers en France* (1932), or those by Wloceski on the Italians and the Poles. We had to wait for the 1960s and the work of Serge Bonnet and Michelle Perrot for a highlighting of the foreign dimension of the working-class population and for questions to be raised on the consequences of the presence of foreign labor and on the xenophobia of the French-born working class and its influence on the organization of workers' parties.

Foreigners have always been discounted both in administrative statistics and during census taking; statistical uncertainty can be explained by the methods of these two heterogeneous sources, both of which naturally tend to neglect immigrants in irregular situations, living at the margins of legality. The Ministry of the Interior adds up the residency cards registered at police stations; therefore, entries into the territory are better known than departures. The census is based upon the declarations of individuals who do not always know their situation vis-à-vis nationality. However, once they become French, there is no way for ordinary surveys to distinguish within the French population those who are of foreign origin. The way in which the Vichy government used such knowledge contributes, moreover, to making any effort in this direction suspect. We cannot help approving the political reasons that prohibit identifying and marking out populations of foreign origin; nevertheless, the result is that we come to know nothing about the pathways of advancement inside French society, and we can only ask questions.

Are there privileged routes of advancement inside French society that differ according to one's country of origin? Have the children of French peasants and of Polish workers, Italian masons, and Jewish craftsmen who have become French citizens known the same channels of social advancement? Do there exist, on the other hand, significant differences between populations from diverse foreign nations and those from various French regions? It is known that people from various regions of France enter different professional sectors in different ways. The North and West for example, supply fewer civil servants (except for Lorraine) than the southern regions of France. Is geographic and social mobility according to region of origin greater or lesser than mobility according to national origin? There again, we are reduced to conjecture.

We do not know with any degree of certainty whether these diverse groups have used in different ways the three privileged routes of social mobility, which are well known to sociologists: starting a business; attending a school in preparation for a career in the civil service; and the riskier, more marginal, but sometimes quicker route of being promoted through sports and entertainment. We can wonder whether in France, too, certain groups either prefer or are made to suffer through the most marginal routes (as American blacks in this century had a reputation for musical talent before getting involved in great numbers in the political arena) while other groups endeavor to penetrate directly the most central sectors of modern life, defined by technical competence (engineers and technocrats) or political participation.

According to some social representations and certain statistical data, the mobility and advancement of French citizens of Italian origin seem to have privileged the creation of small enterprises, particularly in trade and construction and through commitment to left-wing political parties and unions. Jews seem more often to have adopted the academic route and to have penetrated, thanks to it, all state bodies, including the most prestigious. Poles and Spaniards have more often become wage earners in private enterprises. Many sports stars (track and field and soccer) are of Italian, Polish, and North African origin. These are generalizations, gleaned from representations or images, founded upon partial observations that carry a certain grain of truth. But it is unfortunate that they cannot be established definitively by statistics: comparisons between the mobility of the children of Jewish and non-Jewish craftsmen or between the advancement of Italian workers and those of Lorraine in the iron and steel industry would perhaps eliminate belief in the specificity of Jewish and Italian paths of social mobility; it would result, in any case, in invaluable insights about the force of traditions and cultural identities and their evolution in a situation of acculturation.

One can also wonder about the evolution of a classic indicator of integration, the degree of endogamy. This is a difficult issue to the extent that it compares the known rates of marriage inside a group to an abstract or theoretical situation in which each member of the national society is considered equally likely to marry any member of the other sex, a situation that has obviously never existed. In reality, as we have known since the classic book by Alain Girard, a significant tendency toward endogamy exists, because there is a strong likelihood that members of the same social classes and the same regions will intermarry. This raises two questions. First, is endogamy inside immigrant populations both before and after naturalization more pronounced than the endogamy that already exists inside the general French population, in diverse social groups? Second, if this is the case, to what extent does it signal the perpetuation of a particular behavior and the affirmation of a specific identity?

Because of our inability to answer these questions as far as the past is concerned, we are endeavoring to do our best for the present. A working group made up of members of our seminar at the EHESS (Ecole des Hautes Etudes en Sciences Sociales) and of statisticians belonging to the Social Studies division of the INSEE (Institut National de la Statistique et des Etudes Economiques) under the direction of Annie Fouquet reminds us, by its temporary failure, that statistical data are themselves social productions. Our knowledge of foreigners comes from the census, on the one hand, and on the other, from a few large sample surveys, such as the survey *Emploi* (Employment), based on nearly 60,000 households and involving 170,000 individuals. The results of these surveys, as well as some data drawn from administrators and managers in the civil justice and national education bureaucracies, now constitute the main sources of our knowledge of foreigners in France. Foreigners can be identified as such by their own self-declaration, which must inevitably introduce distortions, in particular for those children born in France of foreign parents.[1] Nothing in the population data, however, allows us to distinguish the diverse national or religious origins of French citizens.

Concerning the populations defined by a religion, I have shown elsewhere the difficulties of finding an indicator that permits their identification, since by reason of the principle of secularity of the state, it has not been possible since the 1872 census to ask questions dealing with religious practices and affiliation (*Les limites* 319–32). For populations defined by national origin, we have an acceptable indicator: the birthplace of the grandparents. But there are curious omissions in INSEE's survey, FQP (Formation-Qualification-Profession); it asks questions about the profession of the grandfather but not about his place of birth (INSEE, *Données*). Among the surveys concerning living conditions, *Cumul des inégalités* (Plurality of Inequalities) asks about original nationality, the parents' nationality (in a single item: French/foreigner), and the grandparents' professions (INSEE, *Données*).[2] This kind of sociological research attests to the weight assigned to class and the lack of attention given to the facts of immigration. One hopes that in the future a means of mitigating these insufficiencies can be put into place. However, the introduction of an item that can serve indirectly to mark the subpopulations of foreign origin in the French population would not produce significant results for several years.

3. For Multiculturalism, French Style

The social functions of such lack of knowledge are evident: nothing must be allowed to distinguish native-born French people from others. The systematic organization of this social ignorance is one of the means permitting the maintenance of national unity.[3] Hervé Le Bras and Emmanuel Todd see in the centralization of the French state, in the unity of the language and culture, and in the affirmation of the universality of man and citizen the answer to the anthropological diversity of France. According to them, France, more than any other European country, because of its lack of anthropological unity, has had to fight against centrifugal forces. But how can regional (that is, anthropological) French diversity, which they point out, be separated from that which is due directly to immigration? Are not certain French regions populated mainly by the children and grandchildren of immigrants? Was not this invention of France more necessary to make a single nation out of Belgians, English, Germans, Jews, Italians, Spaniards, and North Africans, who formed the French population, than out of people from Brittany, Limoges, and Lorraine?

That is to say, it is difficult to lightly call into question the political tradition that, in the strong sense of the term, constructed the nation. The forms of multiculturalism that intellectuals have dreamed of, or are dreaming of, in their concern to fight against all forms of racism and to respect all values in the name of cultural relativism can only be introduced in the full awareness of the limits of the possibility of this multiculturalism. In what way can France be pluri- or multicultural? If it is a question of respecting the specificities related to private, religious, and family life, pluriculturalism poses no conflict of principles in a democracy, which, by definition, respects the fundamental principle of the separation of the public and the private; in this sense, France has always been and remains pluricultural. If, on the other hand, it is a question of introducing new forms into public life, altering the rules and obligations of the citizenry can only be limited. France is politically and culturally immersed in the Jacobin tradition; it was founded historically on the equivalence of nationality and citizenship (except in the colonies, where for example, Algerians were nationals without being citizens), and by the tendency toward equating national and cultural unity. The recent decentralization does not contradict this tradition, and the failure of the regionalist movements in the 1970s is, in this respect, significant. France cannot call into question this tradition without calling into question its very existence as a state. No nation can have suicide as a vocation (Schnapper, "Unité nationale").

This said, it must be admitted that the principle of separation of the public and private, conforming to the democratic principle and satisfying in the abstract, is not always easy to put into application, for the very border between the two can be the object of conflict. For example, does the decision of a father to marry a young girl against her will to her unknown cousin in Algeria, in fulfillment of a traditional interpretation of Koranic law, pertain to the public or the private sphere?

Islam poses, in effect, a dilemma with regard to the French national tradition. Koranic rules concerning individual rights not only contradict French common law but are also in conflict with social customs and dominant values. Now it is not possible to envisage a France in which respect for common law is not enforced on populations stably settled, whose children are inclined to become French citizens. Although the Muslim tradition does not recognize the separation of the political and religious spheres, the secularity of the state is a feature of our political tradition. As Rémy Leveau and I have shown elsewhere, while it is desirable that temporary and local accommodations be found to permit Muslim populations to observe the rules of religious Islam and to constitute a representation of Muslims of France independent of foreign Muslim governments (855–84), in the long term, Muslim institutions of culture and worship can only be recognized as private organizations, on the model of other religious communities. The Jewish communities, for example, which at the time of the Revolution commanded a policing power over their members, became private associations, given to worship, to culture, or to charity. To claim that another path of evolution is possible is to give proof of either idealism or bad faith.

As a host country for immigrants, France can have no policy but that of continuing the integration of its foreign populations through its universal institutions. If it is true that schools, the army, the church, and the unions are in crisis, if their actions today carry less conviction and are less efficient than before, they are still, nevertheless, the only means of true acculturation (Schnapper, *La France*). Critical sociology reproaches educational institutions for treating in an equal manner unequal individuals, but treating them unequally would have a more perverse and discriminatory effect that is even more serious. What would classes be when made up exclusively of foreign children? Moreover, the acculturating effect of schools is relayed through media culture, which exposes all to the same language. Particularist and compensating institutions, despite their good will and the efforts of those responsible, have always led to categorizing the populations in question and have excluded them from normal processes. The social policies that distinguish particular cases as the object of the attention and solicitude of specialized agents end up almost inevitably by labeling those whom they endeavor to help and therefore lead, despite all good intentions, to discrimination. As the American example has shown, a systematic policy of quotas introduces lies into social life and in the long term results only in a false equality.

The efforts to be open to other cultures in schools are obviously desirable, both on the intellectual and the symbolic levels: who would not wish, for example, that a rightful place be made in the teaching of history for non-European cultures and points of view? But the teaching of another culture can be desirable only if it completes the inculcation of French culture, which alone gives to children of foreigners the means of participating in the global society without too many handicaps. The culture of origin (which, at any rate, often is not the culture to which foreign-born parents refer in their daily life) cannot replace the teaching offered by the French school, unless the French wish to form second-class citizens. The extreme logic of respect for cultural particularisms is represented by apartheid, which is enough to show the limits that must be imposed on the principle of respect for particularisms in the national context. The reticence, often observed, of numerous North African parents toward the teaching of Arabic and their preference for the teaching of a universal language such as English, which is more immediately profitable, demonstrate that they are conscious of the dangers of folklorization and of the discrimination that every specialized education entails (see Schnapper, *Eduquer*).[4]

Let us not speak of this as cultural genocide. The acculturation of immigrants and the socialization of children and adolescents of foreign origin educated in France are not equivalent, or even analogous, to cultural genocide. We can regret that Yves Montand has apparently forgotten everything of his parents' Italian culture, but that makes no more sense than regretting not being Eskimo. Every acculturation implies by definition not only the acquisition but also the loss of certain traits. To participate fully in a culture excludes, for each individual, the possibility of participation in another culture in the same way, even if one keeps particular, sentimental, and symbolic links with the country of origin of one's parents'. One must beware of the intellectual sin of reification: culture is not a given, once and for all; it is an unfinished product ever renewable in the activity of those who give it life. The North African and Muslim elements are from now on part of French culture; they have the same claims as other regional or national source cultures. Education remains, in a society that is very technically ambitious, the best means (even if, of course, it is not enough) of obtaining equality, if not equality of opportunity.

In France, true multiculturalism is the power to elect a President of the Republic a Jew, Muslim, or Asian who has been a former student of the Ecole Polytechnique and the Ecole Nationale d'Administration.

Notes

Editor's note: This essay was originally published as "Un pays d'immigration qui s'ignore" in *Le Genre Humain,* Spring 1989. We thank Prof. Schnapper and Editions Seuil for permission to translate and reprint it.

1. The main part of this data is presented in a publication of the INSEE (Institut National de la Statistique et des Etudes Economiques), *Les Etrangers en France,* in the series Contours et Caractères, 1986.

2. The other surveys on the living conditions of households do not usually ask for nationality. When they do, the sample is too weak to go beyond a simple opposition of French/foreigner. The same is true for a survey of salary structures based on 20,000 businesses.

3. This explains the position of the Commission nationale de l'informatique et des libertés (National Commission of Computer Science and Freedoms). For questions relating to religion, union participation, and the state of political refugees, the person administering a survey must specify that the answer is optional and must ask for written and signed permission to be able to record it on a roll card. In order for the information to be anonymously used by the statistician, both these steps must be carried out.

4. For an overview of these problems, see *L'Education multiculturelle,* the publication of the Centre pour la recherche et l'innovation dans l'enseignement (CERI), the Center for Research and Innovation in Education.

Works Cited

Bonnet, Serge. *Sociologie politique et religieuse de la Lorraine.* Paris: Armand Colin, 1972.

Bonnet, Serge, Charles Santini, and Jean Barthélemy. "Les Italiens dans l'arrondissement de Briey avant 1934." *Annales de l'Est.* 12 (1962).

CERI (Centre pour la recherche et l'innovation dans l'enseignment). *L'Education multiculturelle.* Paris: CERI, 1987.

Girard, Alain. *Le Choix du conjoint.* 1964. Paris: Presses Universitaires de France, 1974.

Green, Nancy. *Les Ouvriers juifs à la Belle Epoque: le 'Pletzl' de Paris.* Paris: Fayard, 1985.

INSEE (Institut National de la Statistique et des Etudes Economiques). *Données sociales 1990.* Paris: INSEE, 1990. 94–132.

———. *Les Etrangers en France.* Contours et Charactères. Paris: INSEE, 1986.

Le Bras, Hervé, and Emmanuel Todd. *L'Invention de la France.* Paris: Librairie générale française, 1981.

Leveau, Rémy, and Dominique Schnapper, "Religion et politique: juifs et musulmans maghrébins en France." *Revue française de science politique* (December 1987): 855–84.

Long, Marceau. *Etre français aujourd'hui et demain. Rapport sur la nationalité.* Collection "10/18." Paris: Christian Bourgois, 1988.

Mauco, Georges. *Les Etrangers en France.* Paris: Armand Colin, 1932.

Perrot, Michelle. *Les Ouvriers en grève: France 1871–1890.* Paris: Mouton, 1974. See especially 160–80.

Schnapper, Dominique. "Eduquer les enfants de migrants." *Commentaire* 32 (1985–1986): 1202–05.

——. *La France de l'intégration, Sociologie de la nation en 1990.* Paris: Gallimand, 1991.

——. "Les limites de la démographie des juifs de la diaspora." *Revue Française de sociologie* 18 (1987): 319–32.

——. "Unité nationale et particularismes culturels." *Commentaire* 38 (1987): 361–5.

Wloceski, Stéphane. *L'Etablissement des Polonais en France.* Paris: Picard, 1936.

——. *L'Installation des Italiens en France.* Paris, Alcan, 1934.

Diaspora 1:3 1991

"Our Greater Ireland beyond the Seas"

Paul Arthur
University of Ulster at Jordanstown, Northern Ireland

Occasional Papers on the Irish in South Africa. Donald H. Akenson. Gananoque, ON, Canada: Langdale, 1991.

Half the World From Home: Perspectives on the Irish in New Zealand 1860–1950. Donald H. Akenson. Gananoque, ON, Canada: Langdale, 1990.

The concerns of both these books are wider than their titles suggest. Professor Akenson's work on the Irish diasporas of New Zealand and South Africa also deals with the historiography of Irish America, Irish Canada, and, either directly or obliquely, Ireland. Given this scope, his work adds up to a shrewd and highly literate analysis of British historiography as well as the Irish diaspora. At the same time, it emphatically addresses and criticizes the "filiopietistic excesses" of Irish-American historiography—much of which, he informs us, "has become a massive baroque structure built on quicksand" (*Occasional Papers* 12). Finally, these books contribute to his larger attempt to construct a new concept of Anglo-Celtic culture. These important exploratory exercises in the comparative method are rich in style, method, and detail. In the conclusion to his New Zealand study, he enumerates some of the sources and methods he has employed to illuminate ethnic history: "demographic analysis, institutional history, community studies, biographical sketches, and the reading of works of art for their evidentiary value" (*Half the World* 196). All are indeed contained within these pages and enhance our understanding of the Irish diaspora since the nineteenth century.

First and foremost, Akenson is an expert in demolition, which he has turned into an art form. He writes elegantly when criticizing English cultural imperialism or theoretical Marxism's inadequacies in the field of ethnicity. Above all, he employs his considerable forensic skills to challenge the classical view of Irish-American history:

The historical myth holds that the reason that the Irish-Americans were stuck in cities and were not able to reap the boun-

ties of the American heartland, was that the bastard British
forged shackles in the form of cultural and economic limitations that could not be shaken off, even in the New World. . . .
It must have been a great comfort to have been able to blame
the old enemy rather than either the discriminatory structure
of the American republic or one's own self. ("Data" 17)

Conscious of an Irish tendency toward myth-making and self-deception, Akenson suggests that a suitable subtitle for his South African
volume should be *An Inoculation Against Primitive Beliefs*. Brac-
ingly, he reminds us of a primary rule of ethnic historical scholarship: "If the historical evidence that you are assaying confirms what
your grandmother told you, then check, and check again" (*Occasional Papers* 11).

As a result of his own rechecking, he refines and challenges the
accepted wisdom about the Irish diaspora in two important respects.
He writes that the diaspora consists of both Catholics and Protestants—a conclusion that may not surprise the ordinary layperson
but that will come as a shock to some Irish-American academics and
activists. And by highlighting Irish-American mythologies, he allows us to be more sensitive in our handling of the Irish elsewhere.
Drawing on what he calls "two reputable and highly sophisticated
studies" conducted in the 1970s and 1980s[1], he concludes that the
majority of Americans who claimed, in that period, to be of Irish
descent were Protestant and that the Irish ethnic group was polar-
ized between Protestants and Catholics who did not necessarily fit
into received stereotypes. For example, the Catholics who identified
themselves in these studies as being of Irish descent had a significantly higher family income and were less likely to be working class
than the Protestants; they were also twice as likely to be university
graduates. Akenson draws on these studies to illustrate that what
are assumed to be the "facts" simply need not be so.

Armed with that stricture, he examines the South African–Irish
diaspora. It must be said that the two studies under review here are
not precisely analogous, something which Akenson readily admits
(*Occasional Papers* 94). The Irish in South Africa make up no more
than 3 or 4% of the white population. They belong to a privileged
group, possess a relatively low degree of ethnic consciousness, and,
when it suits their purposes, are willing to merge into other ethnic
groups. If we examine the cohort that arrived in the late nineteenth
and early twentieth centuries, three characteristics emerge. They
were mostly Protestant, they came from the more prosperous East
Ulster and Leinster, and they were highly skilled. Unlike their
American counterparts, they had no sense of self-celebration, in that
they did not raise any great memorials to themselves. They distinguished themselves in three areas: the military, the management of

imperialism, and the spread of the capitalist economy. In short, it would be difficult to distinguish these largely Protestant Irish immigrants from their English, Scottish, and Welsh counterparts who settled in South Africa. Akenson makes much of this in his discussion of Anglo-Celtic culture (a topic to which we shall return).

New Zealand presents a more interesting and complex case. Whereas the South African book is a short one of five chapters with a title that self-consciously refers to its "occasional" nature, the New Zealand study is a much larger work, divided into three sections—"The Aggregate Picture," "Methods of Detail," and "Envoi"—whose titles hint at Akenson's idiosyncratic working method. The composite picture that emerges is one of immigrants who had a lower level of skills than other whites and were more rural and less involved with the modernizing world of the industrial revolution. Unlike other groups from the British Isles, Irish immigrants peaked in number in 1886 and declined thereafter, that is, after New Zealand government-aided assistance ceased to provide the "pull" part of the pull-push model that fuels most emigration. Within this broad profile, Akenson sketches a fascinating comparison of Catholic and Protestant immigrants. This representation of the Catholic community is heavily indebted to the work of the novelist Dan Davin, while his portrait of the Protestant community uses a greater diversity of sources.

We are presented with two peoples differing in attitudes and behavior. The Protestants rapidly adapted to the political culture of the colony that in fact they helped to fashion, whereas Catholics appeared to regard their New Zealand not as a distinct polity but rather as a site for the expansion of Irish Catholicism. Unlike their South African counterparts, the New Zealand Irish engaged in forms of self-celebration. While the Protestant culture was neither as robust as the Catholic nor as viable as a separate community, it went on to produce New Zealand national leaders of the caliber of John Ballance and William F. Massey. These men embodied powerful and generally held convictions that tended toward the hegemonic: "The conviction with which they held their Protestantism and their imperial loyalism, the energy with which they adhered to the 'British' way of life, the ability with which they articulated 'British' ideas of government, law and politics, meant that they played a major role in defining the emerging Pakeha consensus which became, eventually, the New Zealand sense of identity" (*Half the World* 158). New Zealand itself was the monument that Irish Protestantism constructed for itself.

Irish Catholics, on the other hand, "were just slightly a people apart" (158). This is hardly surprising. Initially, the New Zealand government was not keen to accept Irish immigrants because it assumed that most would be Roman Catholics, and so it placed as many of its recruiting agents as it could in the more Protestant North of Ireland. (Had it not been for the fact that Ireland had a surfeit of single women prepared to emigrate, it is conceivable that Akenson would have had little material with which to work). As late as the 1960s, there is evidence of anti-Irish attitudes among many New Zealanders. What is not clear is the extent to which this prejudice is constructed by the perception of the Irish Catholics in New Zealand as "slightly a people apart." Akenson traces their ethnic distinctiveness by examining the way in which they developed and maintained their separate educational system. He describes the Roman Catholic religion in New Zealand as a "boundary maintenance system" (*Half the World* 157) and its policy for controlling its school system as "a bonding process, both religious and ethnic in nature" (*Half the World* 169). The pursuit of that policy separated the Catholic Irish from the rest of the population: "From the Victorian era onwards, Catholic church leaders in New Zealand, adopting attitudes and honouring precedents from Ireland, latched on to the school system as the single most important mechanism for preserving the faith, and in so doing they also preserved their ethnic identity" (*Half the World* 159). This distinction between Catholic and Protestant is an important point and calls into question some of Akenson's more general statements about the Irish diaspora.

Before getting into areas of disagreement, I must set out the common ground. In the first place, Irish out-migration is an important and legitimate subject for comparative study. It can, according to Akenson, "legitimately be labelled a diaspora. More than any of the other national cultures in the British Isles, Ireland became an international society. To live in Ireland in the second half of the nineteenth century was always to have the possibility of emigration on one's personal horizon" (*Half the World* 11). Second, Akenson represents accurately the nature of post-Famine Irish Catholicism: "The *growing* adherence to Catholic practice was in large degree a result of the replacement of a traditional Gaelic culture with a quickly modernising world view that involved coming to terms with English-language culture. Catholicism became the bulwark of Irish cultural identity" (*Half the World* 165; emphasis is added). That last sentence is important in the light of some of the author's assertions about the Irish diaspora. Take the statement (which he describes as a "theme—indeed, almost a theory") that "despite their image of being democratic, rebellious and anti-imperialist in general and anti–British Empire in particular, the Irish have actually been among the greatest supporters of the Second British Empire and the Commonwealth" (*Occasional Papers* 30). He cites as evidence a study of the Indian Civil Service between 1855 and 1914: "Of the various Irish responses, Scott argues, the most common, contrary to what most of the literature has stressed, was that of support: a broad category encompassing conscious and active collaboration as well as acquiescence in laws, values and social structures that were partly shaped by British hegemony" (*Occasional Papers* 39). He is critical of "the dominant mythology within Irish historiography [that] emphasizes resistance to empire and virtually ignores collaboration" (*Occasional Papers* 43).

No one can take exception to such remarks as a corrective to "filio-pietistic excesses". Akenson points out, for example, that whereas 150 Irishmen fought on the Boer side in the Second Anglo-Boer War, 28,000 Irish fought on the British side. But here we need to introduce a note of caution. Joining the army was a form of out-migration. It did not necessarily entail an unquestioning loyalty to queen and empire. It was one form of reaction, among many, to what Matthew Arnold called "the despotism of fact," the sheer, grinding poverty of life for so many in nineteenth century Ireland. That reaction took many forms: emigration, rebellion, even escape into the elaboration of language. In his wonderful evocation of Gaelic culture coming to terms with the spread of the English language, the Irish playwright, Brian Friel, describes Irish as a rich language "full of the mythologies of fantasy and hope and self-deception—a syntax opulent with tomorrows. It is our response to mud cabins and a diet of potatoes; our only method of replying to . . . inevitabilities" (Friel act 2, sc. 1, p. 42).

But reaction to the despotism of empire also took the form of collaboration. The radical French historian, Octave Mannoni, argued in 1950 that the colonizer created a neurotic sense of inferiority in the colonized, which he called the Prospero Complex. It took many forms, including imitation as the best form of flattery. One of the most critical studies of modern Irish society has condemned the

> dependency syndrome which had wormed its way into the Irish psyche during the long centuries of foreign dominance. . . . The Irish mind was enveloped in, and to some extent suffocated by, the English mental embrace. This was quite natural. A small occupied country, with an alien ruling class, culturally penetrated by the language and many of the thought processes of the coloniser, was bound in large measure to imitate the example of the powerful and the prosperous. (Lee 627)

Before we rush to brand the Irish diaspora as one of willing imperialists we need, therefore, to put that diaspora in context and to scrutinize it in greater depth. Akenson has conducted that scrutiny by challenging some of the wilder claims of other historians of ethnicity and has drawn a very useful (though broad-brush) distinction between Catholics and Protestants. But he may have gone too far in trying to devise a counter-theory. We get glimpses of it in his introduction of the concept of an Anglo-Celtic culture. We do well to remind ourselves that culture "is one of the two or three most complicated words in the English language. This is so partly because of its intricate historical development, in several European languages, but mainly because it has now come to be used for important concepts in several distinct intellectual disciplines and in several distinct and incompatible systems of thought" (Williams 76–77). Insofar as the Irish had become English-speaking, it was not altogether surprising that they should emigrate to countries where the English language dominated, nor that they should adopt the modes and values of the host country. Akenson (quoting) admits as much in a passage about the South African Irish: "We are not witnessing the mass attraction of bigoted racialists to a segregationalist's dream, rather, we are observing how ordinary people, confronted by a particular social structure, will tend to conform to the attitudes, values, and norms implicit in it" (*Occasional Papers* 45). What I am suggesting is that the concept of Anglo-Celtic culture is so flexible that it can be used to highlight commonalities (the English language) as well as distinctiveness (the role of Irish Catholics in New Zealand's school system). It is a concept that patently does not stand up in the United States and is dubious in New Zealand and Australia but that may, however, fit the South African model, in which we are dealing with a smaller and more homogeneous cohort.

Admittedly, Akenson introduces the term "Anglo-Celtic" as an antidote to "British" or "English" and in that respect he opens up an interesting debate, but it is not one that should be (or is) confined to the "White Commonwealth." For many years now a lively debate has ensued about the nature of the archipelago in the northwest of Europe; most call it the "British Isles," but Irish nationalists are more comfortable with the expression "these islands," and at least one politician has suggested a new acronym: IONA (the Islands of the North Atlantic). From his fastness in Scotland, Tom Nairn may have been the progenitor of this debate, with his gloriously provocative *Break-Up of Britain* and, a decade later, his subversive *Enchanted Glass*. As the titles imply, Nairn was less than happy with the dominance of "Britain" and all that it implied. Hugh Kearney offered some sort of antithesis in his *British Isles*, in which he argued for a "Britannic framework" as "an essential starting point for a fuller understanding of these so-called 'national' pasts" (1). If we are seeking a synthesis, perhaps we should look at the work of J. G. A. Pocock, especially his "Limits and Divisions," where he writes about "the historiography of no single nation but of a problematic and uncompleted experiment in the creation and interaction of several nations" (318).

The marriage of works by Pocock and Akenson could begin to clarify this important debate. The great merit of Akenson's contribution is that in embarking on the journey of demythologizing, he has begun to ask several important questions about the nature of the Irish diaspora. What this review is suggesting is that to understand the latter, we may need to look more closely at the links between the host countries and the developing politics of the mother country. In his conclusion to the New Zealand study, Akenson makes a plea for the larger program of "the necessity of studying demotic culture" (*Half the World* 203). That is a valid point. Ironically, an outcome could be that we will be exporting the Catholic/ Protestant division of Northern Ireland to the very host countries to which many emigrants escaped in part because they wanted to put that division behind them.

Notes

The title of this article is a phrase of James Joyce from *Ulysses* (New York: Random, 1961), 329.

1. The studies were produced by the National Opinion Research Center of the University of Chicago in the 1970s and the Gallup polling organization in the 1980s and are cited in Akenson (*Occasional Papers* 19). The findings will appear startling only to those who assume that mass Irish emigration began among the poor and impoverished Catholics after the Irish Famine of 1845. It ignores the huge wave of Presbyterian immigrants in the eighteenth century. I have developed this more fully in "Diasporan Intervention."

Works Cited

Akenson, Donald H. "Data: What Is Known about the Irish in North America?" *Ireland and Irish-Australia: Studies in Cultural and Political History*. Ed. Oliver MacDonagh and W. F. Mandle. London: Croom Helm, 1986.

Arthur, Paul. "Diasporan Intervention in International Affairs: Irish America as a Case Study." *Diaspora* 1 (1991): 143–62.

Friel, Brian. *Translations*. London: Faber and Faber, 1981.

Kearney, Hugh. *The British Isles: A History of Four Nations*. Cambridge: Cambridge University Press, 1989.

Lee, J. J. *Ireland 1912–1985: Politics and Society*. Cambridge, England: Cambridge UP, 1989.

Nairn, Tom. *The Break-Up of Britain: Crisis and Neo-Nationalism*. London: New Left Books, 1977.

———. *The Enchanted Glass: Britain and its Monarchy*. London: Radius, 1988.

Pocock, J. G. A. "The Limits and Divisions of British History: In Search of the Unknown Subject." *American History Review* 87.2 (1982): 311–36.

Williams, Raymond. *Keywords: A Vocabulary of Culture and Society*. London: Fontana/Croom Helm, 1976.

Transformations of the Sikh Diaspora

Milton Israel
University of Toronto

The Sikh Diaspora: Migration and the Experience Beyond Punjab.
N. Gerald Barrier and Verne A. Dusenberry, eds. Columbia, MO:
South Asia Publications, 1989.

1

Today, many people in the West believe they see in migration an external threat to their cultures and societies no less significant than the Islamic invasions that were stopped at the gates of Vienna in 1529 and 1683. The British have sought to protect themselves from the contemporary challenge by legislating an end to the "open house" ideal of their imperial heyday; with its concentration of alien dress, smells, language, and norms of behavior, an area like Southall has become a symbol of danger to national tradition. In France, the presence of a Muslim North African minority has stimulated a more extreme than usual defense of a presumably endangered French civilization, reflected in increasing votes for right-wing candidates wielding racist rhetoric. The easy inclusion of Algeria, Indochina, and Tunisia into "un terre Français" is the distant memory of an idealistic and apparently naïve past. In Germany, the euphoria over unification has been succeeded by fears of population movements from the east that might create an intolerable economic, social, and cultural burden.

In the decade after World War II, Canada and the United States began the process of removing the racist immigration policies that had protected the presumed purity of their mainstream societies. The response from Asia was immediate; quotas were filled and increased over time. The resulting diasporan communities of Chinese, Indian, Pakistani, and Sri Lankan peoples and the continuing pressure from outside have, however, produced defensive strategizing not unrelated to the recent European response. Legitimate refugees still may not be turned back, but no precise and satisfying definition of a legitimate refugee exists. And we now live in a world where vast numbers of people on the move have no doubt about the legitimacy of their own refugee status. For example, for the Canadians and their cumbersome refugee determination mechanism, economic distress does not qualify a would-be immigrant for refugee status; the danger to life must be based on evidence of political persecution, or a war must be in progress. Yet since anyone who can get to Canadian soil gains all the civil rights of Canadian citizens, lengthy legal struggles become inevitable and endlessly reiterate the confrontation between enlightened ideals and practical self-interest.

In recent history, every generation has encountered a period when its stable world of familiar and comfortable situations has been challenged and the ability to be at home in one's own country apparently has been undermined. Beyond the normal generational confrontation of styles, values, and behavior, individuals both in East and West share today the sense that they dwell in a shifting world that has made a fundamental impact on long-held and carefully defined social relationships and cultural norms. Yet the reality of a dynamic and modernizing Asia has been relatively slow to affect the viewpoint and perspective of Europeans and North Americans; they still do not recognize the extent to which the East, too, is changing. The perceived context of continuing technological and economic dominance on one side and mass impoverishment on the other directs attention to a vast range of peoples ruled by autocrats or corrupt officials, still viewed as benighted and otherworldly. There remains for the West an essential East Asia, India, and tropical Africa, regions that are assumed to be fundamentally different in culture and populated by wretched masses denied control over their own destiny by the legacy of an irrational tradition that in fact increasingly responds to pressures similar to those felt by the West.

2

The rise of Japan as a world economic power has stimulated a slow, partial erosion of such western stereotypes of the East, but understanding has been grudging and selective. Japan began the process of self-revision at the turn of the century, with an alliance with the British that acknowledged Japan's naval power and a subsequent victory in the Russo-Japanese War. Japanese power confronted the West on equal terms in World War II, and the challenge of Japanese expertise currently produces a defensive and respectful Western response. But Japan continues to be thought of as an honorary western country, an eastern player of a western game. Even though workers and managers in the West are learning to play on Japanese terms, generalizations regarding Asian cultures as fertile soil for modern development have been reluctant and rare. Taiwan, Singapore, South Korea, and, more recently, Thailand, Indonesia, and Malaysia have been recognized as modernizing economies and societies, but a nineteenth century worldview retains its influence and represents those countries as participating in a global economy but remaining culturally isolated and different otherwise. Those who travel from West to East go to seek out the exotic or to search for images and reflections of our own imagined past, which we attribute to the West before it became enlightened, progressive, modern, rich, and successful.

It is just this continuing psychic isolation of the West that is now being challenged by the new and far more massive migration from East to West. The quaint Chinatowns that attracted white patrons to restaurants and open markets still exist, but they have now moved from the center to the margin of large and affluent Chinese populations spread throughout major North American cities. There are no longer little Indias reflecting the cloistering in ethnic enclaves of peasant communities called to the new world to work the land and the lumber mills; instead, well-educated and professionally trained South Asians who immigrated in the 1960s and 1970s have moved directly into mainstream jobs and mainstream neighborhoods. The distance—in miles or thousands of miles—that allowed neighborhoods and whole societies to live apart is eroding quickly. The trauma is greater for European societies long used to a broadly shared national history, language, and culture. But the change for North America is also significant. Emma Lazarus's poem enshrined at the base of the Statue of Liberty did not specifically limit America's invitation to whites only, and each generation has had to come to terms with the immigrants who came after. The descendants of English colonists had their problems with northern Europeans, who subsequently were concerned by the massive flow from the impoverished European South and East. And now the children of these Ellis Island graduates confront a situation different only in detail, not in kind. But the cultural distance is or seems especially great because the images, myths, and stereotypes that preceded this Asian passage have left their mark.

In a sentimental and profoundly revisionist context, the United States and Canada have recently been recasting and coming to terms with the nature and significance of turn-of-the-century European immigration. This reconsideration is taking place in the midst of the new wave from Asia, and it has been difficult to cope with both at the same time. The tradition of five or six young men from Italy or Ukraine crowding into a tiny flat to begin their life in America has become a source of pride for their successful descendants. Textbooks have been revised, and photographic exhibitions and coffee table books about European immigration in the period from 1880 to 1924 attract a large and growing market. But a similar group of Sri Lankan refugees is perceived only as destroying buildings and neighborhoods, adding to the public cost, and threatening a way of life. In this case, it is temporal distance that makes acceptance easier; it is easier to come from immigrant stock than to be an immigrant, at any time.

But the renewed immigrant flow has served a practical purpose. The earlier assimilationist ideal, combined with the domination of immigrants by host culture identity and behavioral norms, had long suppressed the reality of the role and place of twentieth century immigrants in North America, as they moved into and participated in the building of these societies. Even those who had language, educational, and social skills were absorbed on the host society's terms. Those who did not have such skills continued to live as hyphenated peoples with identities informed by stereotyping as harsh as that applied to Asians today. But the environment is changing. Spanish language signs are now common in the United States. School history curricula are being recast to reflect the range and variety of immigrant participation. In Canada, multiculturalism has become a powerful symbol and steering agent for the mobilization of public support for a pluralistic view of Canadian society and identity.

How the national societies of North America and Europe will evolve and change remains unclear, but the extraordinary contemporary phenomena that Arjun Appadurai describes as "global cultural flows" need to be understood at a range of levels, from the adaptation-stereotypes of the individual immigrant to the international relationships of distant states that have been affected in new ways by this transfer of people. The literature on immigration is large, but it remains too dependent on either theory and generalization or, at the other extreme, on parochially narrow community studies. As scholars we need to be concerned with those elements of our own cultural baggage that inform and guide perspective. We need to involve our subjects in the creative process of the research enterprise. We need to make more discriminating judgments about responses that may reflect particular ethnic traits and traditions and those that are a product of the immigrant situation widely shared with others. To accomplish this, we must venture into comparative research, both among different ethnic groups and among different communities of diasporan nations. We need to use sources, especially official sources, more critically and to seek out new materials, such as oral testimony, that are often more difficult to use. For those who are concerned with Asian immigration, we need above all to work on both sides of the water, alone if we have the skills or, if we do not, in association with those who do. The view from North America of the Asian "push" factors which stimulated immigration or of the continuing impact of emigration on the home society is unavoidably distorted and limited. And the supposition that diaspora life and the process of adaptation to the challenges of a host society are separate in some absolute way from family and society in their home territory is particularly erroneous for this generation of immigrants. Kinship linkages have been internationalized in a continuing flow in both directions of people, information, ideas, and viewpoints.

3

The need for these imperatives, as well as the usefulness of observing them, is made evident by the book under review, which focuses on one group of recent immigrants from Asia. *The Sikh Diaspora: Migration and the Experience Beyond Punjab* brings together the work of most of the major scholars involved in this field. Virtually every aspect of Sikh diasporan life is considered, as are the historical and ongoing roles of the Punjab context. In addition, the essays address major historiographical and ideological issues that have made this a controversial field in recent years. Both the ideal of Sikh Panth unity and the reality of competition and division are analyzed in detailed case studies. The "myth of return" and the process of change from sojourner to settler are described and analyzed from a range of perspectives and in a number of settings. Fundamental questions that associate contemporary scholarship in the West with current social, religious, and political issues in Punjab are considered: Who is a Sikh? How is one to be a good Sikh in the diaspora? What is identifiably Sikh about the Sikh response to diasporan challenges? While references are made to Sikh communities in East Africa and Asia, these essays primarily concern major diaspora settings in Britain, the United States, and Canada. The widely shared political and social traditions of these host societies are considered to be a sound base for productive comparative studies; in fact, there is a general concern noted in many of these essays about the need to work in a comparative context, both within these diaspora societies and in the Punjab homeland. There is a recognition that the literature and the field are still quite small, but there is a sense of coming of age and the need to refine easy judgments and generalizations.

It is appropriate that H. W. McLeod should set the context and raise the fundamental questions in his introductory essay. As the doyen of western scholars of the Sikh experience, he has played a primary role in internationalizing interest and research. At the same time, he has been at the center of the conflict between western scholarship and traditional Sikh hagiography that has resulted from his enterprise. McLeod notes the continuing "uncertainties" in the historical record and urges scholars to challenge, as he does, easy generalizations regarding the beginnings of Sikh immigration and the reasons for the movement beyond Punjab. The significance of financial necessity as a primary push factor needs to be reconsidered, in his view, in the context of the role of *izzat* (pride, honor, status) in determining a decision to emigrate. He argues that, rather than a concern for possible impoverishment, it was the need to maintain and enhance an already affluent family's position that stimulated the sending of sons abroad.

In addition to raising such fundamental issues, which have made his work both controversial and intellectually stimulating, McLeod insists that "we can expect to encounter a problem" of distinguishing Sikh from Hindu. He connects this concern, which is now at the center of a continuing confrontation in Punjab, to the diaspora experience, noting that in talking about "Sikh" immigration, we have chosen "an imprecise adjective." A "Punjab" exodus that seems to have included both Sikhs and Hindus may yet emerge as the best description of the early years of migration. This theme and others revised by McLeod are taken up in more detail in subsequent chapters. In particular, McLeod notes the continued dominance of an interpretation of Sikh identity established during a period of dynamic revivalism in the last quarter of the nineteenth century and the early decades of the twentieth century. His questioning of this legacy has set the research agenda concerning Sikh identity, cultural adaptation, and fear of cultural loss, both in Punjab and in the diaspora.

For many Sikh writers, McLeod is part of the problem, as are other western and western-trained scholars whose work challenges traditional interpretation and identity. The politicized nature of contemporary debate is reflected in the confrontational context of relations between these two groups. Migration has created an international Sikh Panth and made Sikhism an international religion, one result of which has been this dynamic scholarly enterprise: for some it is a reflection of vitality and renewal, while to others it is a source of danger and loss.

N. G. Barrier provides a review of the major elements of the Singh Sabha period of Sikh cultural revitalization, noting that it was also a period of significant overseas migration. Whereas McLeod argues that the majority of early migrants were "little affected by its ideas," Barrier emphasizes the development of communication networks within both Punjab and the diaspora, as well as between them. He describes the establishment of institutions and the role of leaders and missionaries working in a defensive context in order to meet the perceived Hindu challenge by asserting a distinctive Sikh identity. The essential aspects of that identity, as defined by the chief Khalsa Diwan (the central institution of the Singh Sabha movement), Barrier argues, were definite regarding the distinction from Hinduism, but tolerant and doctrinally accommodative in regard to the range of viewpoints within the Sikh Panth.

In the diaspora communities being established in Canada and the

United States, Barrier describes a recognition of the value of the revitalized Sikh identity in Punjab; such communities call for preachers from Punjab and establish their own Singh Sabha with ties to the chief Khalsa Diwan. There are connections as well between newspapers and journals in Punjab and those outside, adding knowledge of current affairs, ideas, and values to the remittances that had earlier been the major element of connection and exchange. But Barrier insists that there was no transfer of "a fixed and rigid orthodoxy" from homeland to diaspora. He shares McLeod's skepticism regarding the existence of any consensual identity: "Punjabi Sikhs were not united in terms of doctrine or social attitudes, and neither were Sikhs abroad." In fact, he notes, the old divisions of opinion about Jat/non-Jat (caste) and Sahajdhari/Keshdhari (cut or uncut hair) were transferred abroad.

Verne Dusenberg's contribution also deals with attempts to objectify Sikh doctrine and practice and with the desire to establish a monolithic code of essential beliefs. He notes that the effort to achieve a definitive united identity is an "on-going process" both in the Punjab and the diaspora. Dusenberg provides descriptions and analyses of three disputes in Canada and the United States as examples of the continuing—now transnational—debate. In the first case, converted Gora (white) Sikhs have asserted the absolute necessity of wearing the "five K's" for anyone who wishes to be considered a Sikh. In a fundamental challenge to many Sikh immigrants from Punjab and their descendants, they have insisted that those who do not live a "Sikh life" are not Sikh. Their challenge has included such issues as the subjugation of women and caste consciousness, as well as the cutting of hair and the wearing of religious symbols. While many discount their extreme orthodox position, the Goras have been successful in dramatizing and publicizing an important element in this continuing debate.

A second example concerns a dispute in the oldest Sikh institution in North America, the Khalsa Diwan Society in Vancouver. A westernized businessmen's faction that had played a major role in building a new gundwara and had controlled its management was challenged by representatives of a more recent and more orthodox wave of immigrants from the Punjab. The confrontation—sometimes violent—continued throughout the 1960s and 1970s, and eventually, in a secret ballot, the old guard (representing adaptation and assimilation) was routed, and the orthodox faction took control.

In a final example, Dusenberg describes the orthodox perception of a parallel, dual threat of Hindu reabsorption in India, on the one hand, and accommodation with western society in the diaspora, on the other. He also notes the continuing clash between western historiographic methods and Sikh hagiography and describes in particular the debate that has arisen from McLeod's work concerning

Guru Nanak's relationship to the North Indian Sant tradition, the role of the Jat influx in shaping Sikh practices, and the persistence of caste in the Sikh Panth. Dusenberg insists that there is a profound misconception regarding McLeod's aims and that there is no "foreign threat" determined to undermine the Sikh religion. But those who are confident that a precise and monolithic Sikh identity and doctrine have existed for centuries and that Sikh unity is challenged only by outsiders and backsliders perceive a dangerous challenge in western scholarship anyway.

Karen Leonard adds her voice to the identity debate, insisting that the early twentieth century immigrant community in California was a Punjabi and not specifically a Sikh diaspora. "To go back and emphasize Sikhs and Sikhism," she argues, "does violence to the historical experiences of the immigrants and their descendants." Based on a range of interviews, her work describes the confrontation with a racist social environment as well as the isolation from any significant contact with their source (home) culture, which stimulated a process of adaptation and an assimilationist ideal among those pioneers: they removed their turbans, cut their hair, married Mexican wives, and encouraged their children to become Americans.

Leonard notes that the term "Hindu" was generally accepted as appropriate when used by members of the host majority, and among Indians—Sikh, Hindu, and Muslim—virtually all relationships crossed religious lines. Knowledge regarding Punjab was passed from Punjabi husband to Mexican wife and to their children, producing an eclectic sense of identity informed as well by the continuing racial bias of the host society. As in the case of the Vancouver Khalsa Diwan Society debate described by Dusenberg, the situation changed dramatically in California with the second wave of Sikh migration, beginning in the 1960s. These people brought with them Sikh consciousness and identity, informed by the trauma of partition in 1947 and by increasing politicization and defensiveness in the 1980s. In this small California community with its unique experience, the reality and legitimacy of the diasporan past has been rejected or ignored recently, in what amounts to a rejection of complexity.

Norman Buchignani and Doreen Indra have dealt with the Sikh experience of racism in the West, the nature of the host systems that promulgated those views, how such views changed over time, and how the Sikhs responded. In this context, they argue the need for comparative studies that will help to clarify what is specifically Sikh about those responses and what is the product of an immigrant situation shared with other groups. In regard to the Sikh response, Buchignani and Indra note examples of situational influence widely shared with other groups. But they also describe particular Sikh perspectives and actions, such as a tendency to unite temporarily and confront aggressively an external challenge of the sort that Japanese and Chinese immigrants might well allow to pass or resolve with more accommodating strategies. Sikhs are especially concerned about izzat, their pride and honor, and any act that appears to offend the community receives a strong response. It is for this reason, these scholars argue, that Canadian immigration constraints were challenged. This essay compares the situation in the early decades of the century with that since the 1960s. The unity of a tiny beleaguered group in the early days is contrasted with the vast and divided community of Sikhs in contemporary Canada. They note the inability of Sikhs to establish effective organization and leadership within large urban centers or at the national level: "What a few thousand Sikhs could once do, 130,000 today cannot." And it is this division that exacerbates the difficulty in determining what is Sikh about Sikh behavior in the diaspora.

James Chadney reviews the history of Sikh immigration and settlement in Vancouver and the formation of an "ethnic community." Through an analysis of the Sikh experience, he seeks to establish an explanatory model of the process of diasporan community-formation. In describing this phenomenon, Chadney rejects the primacy of an external boundary. Rather, he concentrates on adaptation in stages, over time. Beginning with the initial immigration, which fundamentally altered the social environment, Chadney then describes a second stage in which challenges from the host society forced individuals into a group, which then began the process of institutionalizing ethnic boundaries. In a third stage, competition within those boundaries informed community life, providing a basis for a fourth stage of adaptation to the new environment. Chadney's work may provide a useful model for diaspora scholarship. However, it remains at this stage only an outline for further investigation.

Roger Ballard's study of Sikhs in Britain forcefully rejects the existence—in the present as in the past—of any united Sikh Panth. Disunity, he insists, is characteristic of every Sikh community. He describes the sources of factionalism in caste and class and the role of individual charismatic leadership; together, these have entrenched a powerful sectarian element in the political life of Punjab and beyond Punjab, as well. Ballard describes the distinctive development of Jat, Bhatta, and Ramgarhia Sikh life in Britain, noting that the change from a sojourner perspective informed by the "myth of return" to a settler commitment and the establishment of family life produced a "new Punjab" setting in Britain, in which traditional struggles regarding izzat, kin competition, and loyalty were replicated.

In addition to such divisions, new class distinctions resulting from the academic success of some groups and individuals have been added to this complex mix. Bhatras and Ramgarhias, traditionally inferior in ritual status, are often more affluent than their Jat core-ligionists. This has added a new dimension to their traditional strategy of cultural conservatism. They tend to emphasize orthodox practices in dealing with Jats. Generational differences have added an additional element to the debate. Traditional strategies and identities have increasingly less significance for the children of these competitors, who have no personal memory of Punjab. But they will participate in the debate about who is a Sikh, what is the Panth, and what is the nature of Sikh doctrine. Ballard concludes his essay on an optimistic note. Despite and also because of the factionalism, he suggests, Sikhs have made substantial collective achievements. In the extraordinary range and influence of their institutions and community services, they have built an infrastructure that provides an important context for working out their destiny together.

One of the most distinctive Sikh groups noted by Ballard is that which emigrated first to East Africa and subsequently to Britain. Parminder Bhachu's paper concentrates on these "twice removed" Sikhs whose identity and perspective have been determined by lives spent in Uganda and Kenya, not India. Few of the generalizations that apply to the majority of British Sikhs seem appropriate for this group. Their attachment to India has been diminished or eliminated by 70 years of making their lives in another place. For them, there is no "myth of return" to a land that is no longer considered home. Neither are there significant connections to family or kin living in India, or loyalty to a tradition of competition and struggle connected to such relationships.

Their lives as skilled workers and middle-level government servants allowed them to prosper in East Africa and prepared them for a relatively easy resettlement in the United Kingdom after their forced emigration in the 1960s. Bhachu notes that the majority of Jat Sikhs remain working class, in contrast to those East Africans who were able to use their mainstream skills and experience to move into middle-class lives. In addition, because they are overwhelmingly one caste, Ramgarhias have been able to retain cultural and community cohesion and, at the same time, to separate naturally from the Jat majority. In Britain, as Ballard has noted, they tend to emphasize orthodox tradition in identity and doctrine, but from an entrenched and comfortable East African base. They are, therefore, both proponents of an orthodox vision of Sikh unity and a distinctive group reflecting the divisions that seem endemic in Sikh society.

The final essays in this book, by Bruce LaBrack and Arthur Helweg, concern the significance and growing impact of diasporan activity on affairs in India, especially in Punjab. La Brack describes the evolution of a group of "new patrons," who have the resources and desire to make an impact on the academic, political, and social life of their homeland. He notes the efforts of the early sojourners in California, who assumed they would return to their Punjab homes and carefully maintained their connections with them through remittances of substantial portions of very small incomes. While the economic impact was not great, the pattern was established. As McLeod has noted, and LaBrack reiterates, even small remittances served the important social purpose of enhancing their izzat and that of their families. Marriage potential, influence in the village, and the possibility of additional immigration were all affected by this internationalization of the kinship network.

La Brack notes that even those meager funds diminished as sojourners became settlers and began to invest a larger portion of their savings in California. The tradition of relating izzat to a connection with Punjab continued, but gifts to appropriate causes such as the building of a gundwara or support for the Ghadan Party and the Indian nationalist struggle might be substituted for a simple remittance. As is the case in all areas of Sikh diaspora life in North America, the massive increase in Sikh immigration and settlement since the 1960s has had a significant impact on the flow of remittance funds to Punjab.

La Brack recognizes the difficulty in achieving much precision in estimating the amount and impact of this transfer of resources. He insists, however, that it is substantial and has been underestimated. Using 1981 data, he estimates that approximately $2 billion of remittance income flows to India each year and that, of this, about $5 million goes to Punjab. A range of other expatriate investments adds substantially to those amounts. La Brack notes that the Green Revolution tended to benefit those Punjab families who were already in a dominant position in terms of wealth and land ownership. Migrant remittances, he argues, tended to enhance their separation from the less advantaged small farmers. It was the large, successful families who had sent their sons out beyond Punjab who came to control the majority of the land. They had the resources to buy machinery and new seed, to educate their children, and to benefit from new ideas. "Remittances from Sikhs abroad are intertwined and involved with the process of modernization and mechanization in the Punjab," he asserts. It is only the extent of the impact, La Brack argues, that is unclear.

In addition to the obvious economic benefits, La Brack also notes the negative legacy of diasporan activity in the homeland. Inflation, loss of land by marginal farmers, rising unemployment, out-migration, and social instability are at least in part the result of such external influence. The new patrons from the little Punjabs in the West are often resented rich cousins, however creative and useful their role has been.

Arthur Helweg has dealt with another aspect of the impact of diaspora Sikhs on India. He describes the evolution of the separatist campaign and of the idea of Khalistan in the diaspora, long before it emerged as a major phenomenon in India. The Sikh separatist struggle was "primarily an emigrant endeavor," Helweg notes, until the rise to prominence of Bhindranwale in 1982. Yet even in the diaspora, support was limited to a small minority until the Indian attack on the Golden Temple, the death of Bhindranwale, and the subsequent assassination of Indira Gandhi drove increasing numbers of Sikhs and Hindus into newly politicized and confrontational segregation. The destruction of Air India Flight 182 in 1985 entrenched the separation for those who assigned blame to the Sikhs. Canada has been assumed to be the center of the Khalistani cause, and overseas activity has continued to support separatism with both rhetoric and resources. As a result, India's relations with Britain, the United States, and Canada have been affected, as has Sikh identity and reputation within those host societies.

This volume of essays grew out of a 1986 conference held at the University of Michigan. The participants included virtually all of the major scholars working in the field. Many of the arguments and issues included here will be familiar to those who know the literature of this small area of scholarship; these themes have been extended and reiterated in other works. But the collective impact of this volume remains significant. Many of the questions raised remain unanswered. The confrontational controversies remain unresolved. And for those interested in other diaspora communities or the diaspora experience generally, the Sikhs beyond Punjab have a story to tell that must be heard.

Notes on Contributors

Andrew Apter is assistant professor of anthropology at the University of Chicago. He is the author of *Black Critics and Kings: The Hermeneutics of Power in Yoruba Society* and is working on a new project, *"Festac* (Festival of African Culture) for Black People: Oil Capitalism and the Spectacle of Culture in Nigeria."

Paul Arthur is senior lecturer in politics at the University of Ulster at Jordanstown in Northern Ireland. He has written a number of books and articles on the politics of Ireland and is completing a book on contemporary Anglo-Irish relations.

Gillian Bottomley is associate professor of anthropology and comparative sociology at Macquarie University in Sydney, Australia. Her book *From Another Place: Migration and the Politics of Culture* will be published soon. She is coeditor, with M. de Lepervanche and J. Martin, of *Intersexions: Gender, Class, Culture, Ethnicity.*

Arif Dirlik is professor of history at Duke University. His most recent books are *Anarchism in the Chinese Revolution* and, with Ming Chan, *Schools into Fields and Factories: Anarchists, Guomindang, and the Labor University in Shanghai, 1927–32.*

Milton Israel is professor of history at the University of Toronto in Canada and teaches in the Center for South Asian Studies, of which he was formerly director. He recently coedited *South Asians in Ontario,* a special issue of *Polyphony,* and is coeditor with N. K. Wagle of the forthcoming book *Ethnicity, Identity, Migration: The South Asian Context.* He has also edited a book on Nehru and has a book in press on propaganda and the press in the Indian nationalist struggle.

Hamid Naficy teaches in the Department of Film and Television at UCLA and writes on television, cinema, popular culture, and exile. He has just coedited a special triple issue of *Quarterly Review of Film and Video* (13: 1–3, 1991) on "Discourses of the Other: Postcoloniality, Positionality, Subjectivity." His book *Iranian Popular Culture and Television in Exile* will be published in 1993.

Dominique Aron Schnapper is professor of sociology at the Ecole des Hautes Etudes en Sciences Sociales in Paris. She has written some 60 articles and six books, two on the French administrative system, two on acculturation and daily life in Italy, and one on Italian immigration to France. Her study of Jews in France was translated and published in the United States in 1983 as *Jewish Identities in France: An Analysis of Contemporary French Jewry*. She has lectured in the United States and advised the French government on immigration and integration.

David Scott is assistant professor of anthropology at Bates College. His dissertation was on "Yaktovil: The Cultural Poetics of a Minor Sinhala Practice." His articles have appeared in *Economy and Society* and *Dialectical Anthropology* and are forthcoming in *Comparative Studies in Society and History* and *Cultural Anthropology*.

Information for Authors

Diaspora welcomes essays that explore the concepts and practices underpinning the terms contained in its semantic domain: "nation," "exile," "transnational," "multicultural," "ethnic," and others. We solicit essays on all
aspects of the infranational and transnational phenomena now challenging
the homogeneity of the nation-state, including nomadic ideas, works of art,
and mass media productions that traverse frontiers and borderlands. The
journal welcomes studies of specific diasporan communities, existing or
emerging, whether in the First, Third, or Second worlds (e.g., Turks in
Germany; Armenians and Crimean Tatars in the former USSR; Jews, Chinese, and Ukrainians in Canada; Afro-Caribbeans in the UK). It invites
contributions from the disciplines of cultural studies, history, literature,
sociology, religious studies, political science, art history, anthropology, musicology, psychology, economics, and linguistics.

Manuscript preparation. Manuscripts should be typewritten with wide
margins on 8½ × 11 inch bond paper. All material should be double-spaced,
including notes, works cited, extracts, poetry and figure legends. Do not
divide words at the ends of lines. Each section of the manuscript should
begin on a separate line. Assemble the sections in the following order: title
page, text, notes, works cited, figure legends. Acknowledgments should appear as the first unnumbered note. Ordinarily, contributions should not
exceed 40 standard typewritten pages.

In general, the journal follows the recommendations of the *MLA Style
Manual,* including parenthetical documentation with author's name, page
number, and short title if necessary, keyed to works cited. Articles should
have endnotes and works cited.

The journal encourages the submission of suitable illustrations. Photo-
copies are acceptable for first review, but high-quality glossy prints must
accompany the final manuscript. On a separate sheet please provide a legend for each figure. Illustrations will be cropped and sized by the publisher.

Authors are responsible for obtaining permission to reprint extracts and
reproduce illustrations. Copies of permission forms should be supplied with
the final manuscript. All necessary credits and acknowledgments should be
included in the figure legends.

Manuscript submissions. Authors should submit an original and two
copies of their manuscripts to the executive editor, Professor Khachig
Tölölyan, *Diaspora: A Journal of Transnational Studies*, Wesleyan University, Middletown, CT 06459-0100, USA. Authors may request that their
submissions be forwarded to referees anonymously. Essays in French,
Spanish, and German may be submitted; if accepted, they will be translated. Manuscripts cannot be returned unless accompanied by a stamped,
self-addressed envelope.

D I A S P O R A

A JOURNAL OF TRANSNATIONAL STUDIES

For millennia, empires and nation-states persecuted, tolerated, or welcomed the traditional diasporas: Jewish, Greek, and Armenian. Recently, new polities ranging from the African-American and Ukrainian-Canadian to the Chinese-American, the Quebecois, and the Palestinian have entered the semantic domain diasporas share with exile and ethnic communities, immigrants, expatriates, refugees, guest workers, and others. *Diaspora: A Journal of Transnational Studies* is a forum for the analysis of the contending "others" that pose cultural, political, and economic challenges to the hegemony and homogeneity claimed by many nation-states. The journal covers the entire range of phenomena encompassed by various uses of "transnationalism" including movements of people, such as massive migrations that traverse porous frontiers, and movements of capital, technology, and mass media productions that complicate the meanings and consequences of multiculturalism.

Diaspora is an international and interdisciplinary journal that addresses these phenomena as they have functioned since antiquity and in the context of emergent global systems. It publishes contributions from the disciplines of history, literature, political science, cultural studies, anthropology, religious studies, sociology, economics, linguistics, psychology, and musicology. Because nation, diaspora, and transnationalism are contested concepts, the journal offers a forum for debate about the past and present theoretical foundations of these terms.

Diaspora has received First Place recognition in the category of Best New Journal in the 1991 Council of Editors of Learned Journals International Awards Competition.

Subscription Order Form

*Please enter my one-year subscription to Diaspora,
Volume 2, 1992 (3 issues):*

☐ Individuals: $24.50   ☐ Institutions: $49.00
☐ Outside US: $34.50   ☐ Outside US: $59.00

Add $5 for air-expedited delivery, available to countries outside the US only.

Name

Address

City/State/Zip

*Send order with payment to the Journals Department, Oxford University Press,
2001 Evans Road, Cary, NC 27513. For credit card orders (Mastercard, VISA, and American Express are
accepted), include account number, expiration date, and signature.*   JR92